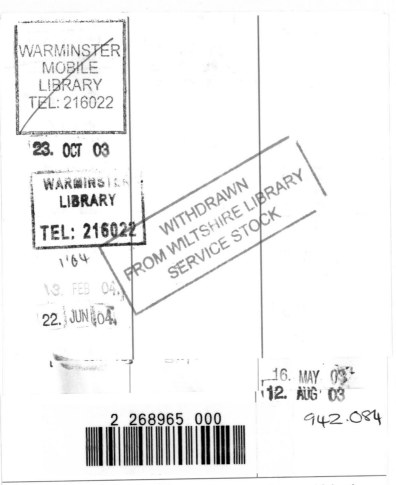

The Life and Times of
GEORGE VI

The Life and Times of
GEORGE VI

Keith Middlemas

Introduction by Antonia Fraser

Book Club Associates, London

To my wife

Series designed by Paul Watkins
Layout by Juanita Grout

Filmset by Keyspools Limited, Golborne, Lancs.
Printed and bound in Great Britain by
Morrison & Gibb Ltd, London & Edinburgh

Contents

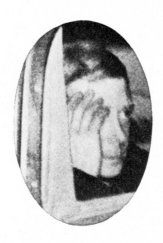

Introduction

IT IS IMPOSSIBLE not to be moved by the life story of King George VI. The combination of adversity in early life, tragedy in his middle years – for so he would have regarded the Abdication crisis – and heroic fortitude which enabled him to overcome both and lead his country successfully during a savage global war, is poignant enough. In human terms, it is even more compelling that the long struggle virtually wore him to his grave, so that far from enjoying a mellow peace after his labours, he died prematurely in 1952 at the age of only 56.

Perhaps the contrast of his early humble expectations with his later career is best seen in his relative positions at the start of the First and Second World Wars. In August 1914 the eighteen-year-old Albert (as he was christened), the second son of George V, was a mere midshipman keeping watch somewhere in the North Sea. On September 3 1939, now King George VI, he recorded in his diary: 'Today we are at war again and I am no longer a midshipman in the Royal Navy . . . the country is calm, firm and united behind its leaders, resolved to fight until liberty and justice are once again safe in the world.' And as the war proceeded, among those leaders, the King came increasingly to symbolise this national unity which he himself had so prized from the outset.

Certainly nothing existed in the Prince's youth to prepare him for the royal position he was one day unexpectedly to occupy. Ever in the shadow of his brilliant elder brother, the popular and dazzling Prince of Wales, he was even plagued by gastric troubles which probably sprang from the neglect of a nurse in infancy who had concentrated on the older child. With the martinet George V and the unbending Queen Mary for parents, it was hardly surprising that he was considered at thirteen to be the most nervous candidate ever interviewed for the Royal Navy. Above all, he was crippled by a stammer, the consequences of which might have been far-reaching, but for the confidence given to him by his beloved wife, and the work of an Australian speech therapist. Doggedly, as Duke of York, he fought to create his own niche in the royal hierarchy, concentrating on those areas such as his celebrated Boys' Clubs where he felt some practical benefits could be spread, and earning from the newspapers the nickname of the Industrial Prince. It was from these sound but quiet beginnings that he discovered the strength which was to make his reign the undoubted success it was in royal terms.

But of course, fascinating as it may be, the development of the King's personality is not the whole story. This was the reign after all which included the sweeping work of the 1945–51 Socialist government, and the other momentous events of our post-war history such as the handing-over of India, and the challenge of the Cold War. The relationship of the King to his Labour ministers is thus of peculiar interest: on the one hand, as Keith Middlemas says, his social ideals fitted with theirs, and on the other he belonged irreparably to a vanished or at any rate fast-vanishing social era. Keith Middlemas, author of a masterly biography of Edward VII in this series, here displays the same excellent grasp of the social and political background essential to our understanding of the reign – and the man – as a whole.

Antonia Fraser

Acknowledgments

Photographs and illustrations are supplied by, or reproduced by kind permission of the following. The pictures on page *14*, 16, 19, 24, 27, 28, 31t, 74, *95* are reproduced by gracious permission of HM the Queen; Associated Press: 34–5; Camera Press: 99, 120t, City of Coventry Libraries: 137; Cooper Bridgeman Library: *94*; Eastern County Newspapers: 207; John Frost: 86, 111; Guildhall Library: 21; Illustrated London News: *82*, *83*; Imperial War Museum: 37r, 41, 145, 148; Keystone Press: 70, 76, 105, 113, 118, 119, 152–3, 155, 158, 190, 204, t & b, 208, 209; London Museum: *3*; National Maritime Museum: *176* t & b; National Portrait Gallery: *15*, *180*; Paul Popper: 13, 23, 50, 51, 56, 60, 61, 63, 65, 69, 77, 78, 81, 88–89, 91, 102–103, 104, 108, 122–3, 125, *126* t & b, *127* t & b, 149, 150, 163, *192*, 173, 183, 184, 185, 187, 191, 194–5, 201, 212, 214 t & b, 215 t & b, 216, 217; Radio Times Hulton Picture Library: 10–11, 20, 31b, 38–39, 43, 44, 46, 59, 62, 66, 67, 71, 73, 79, 93, 110, *114*, *115*, 120b, 128, 133, 167, 170–1, 175, *189*, 190, 197, 198, 200; Royal Air Force College, Cranwell: 37b; Royal Naval College, Greenwich: *2*; Tate Gallery (Henry Moore): 140b; Topix: 156; Walker Art Gallery: 140t.

Numbers in italics refer to colour illustrations.

Picture research by Pat Hodgson.

The author owes acknowledgment to the following for quotations: Sir John Wheeler-Bennett, *George VI* (1958), Macmillan, London and Basingstoke; Paul Channon, '*Chips*' – *The Diary of Sir Henry Channon* (1967), Weidenfeld and Nicolson; Lord Davidson: *Memoirs of a Conservative* (1969), Weidenfeld and Nicolson.

1
Prince Albert
1895–1918

WHEN THE DUCHESS OF YORK gave birth to her second son, on 14 December 1895, at York Cottage, Sandingham, it was a bad day in the family calendar, for it was the anniversary of the Prince Consort's death forty-four years before. Queen Victoria, the baby's great-grandmother, had shown little sign of abating her grief for her late husband, and her children and grandchildren feared a certain displeasure at the omen. The Duke of York was careful, therefore, to forestall any wrath at Osborne when he wrote to ask the Queen to be godmother, and he suggested tactfully that the boy might be called Albert.

The great *materfamilias* was pleased: with sound sense and a wistful reflection on her own toilsome childbearing, she replied: 'Let me express my joy at dear Mary's doing so well and recovering so quickly. Thank God she is very strong. She gets through these affairs like nothing. It is a great satisfaction that it should be a second boy. ...' The letter was accompanied by a bust of the Prince Consort, not only a christening present but a special sort of family blessing. Congratulations flowed in from her many descendants, and the child was duly christened, in February, with godparents to witness to the ties of blood which bound the British monarchy to most of the other royal families of Europe: the Empress Frederick (mother of Kaiser Wilhelm II), the Grand Duke and Duchess of Mecklenburg-Strelitz, the Crown Prince of Denmark, the Duke of Connaught and Prince Adolphus of Teck.

Eighteen months separated Albert Frederick Arthur George – Bertie to his family – from his elder brother Prince Edward. As second son, he would grow up to a different sort of training and very different responsibilities, though the pessimistic might have noted that his father had also been a second son, projected to the position of heir presumptive on the death of the Duke of Clarence in 1892. However, while Queen Victoria lived, the succession of her great-grandchildren seemed infinitely remote; below that apex of the family, feared as well as respected, came first the Prince of Wales, later Edward VII, and lower in the pyramid the Duke of York, later George V. The latter had been jolted by the death of his elder brother out of the naval career which he loved, but there seemed no reason why the new Prince Albert should not follow him in due course into a profession

honoured by royalty, and pass his life as befited a royal duke
in a blend of public duty and private enjoyment of a status and
prestige without equal in Europe.

In the settled world of the 1890s, monarchy seemed actually
to be in the ascendant, notably in Germany, where Queen
Victoria's grandson Wilhelm II was engaged in extending both
his personal power and the international prestige of his country.
The rivalries and tensions to which German economic and

political expansion gave rise, like the beginning of Britain's decline as the greatest of European powers, were beyond the scope of kings to affect, but at least until 1910 the Kaiser and Edward VII believed and behaved as if they could. The power of royal wealth and tradition appeared unbreakable and while, unlike the Kaiser, Edward behaved with complete constitutional propriety, he could also state with equal confidence – '*Mon metier à moi c'est d'être roi.*' Free for over twenty years from republican agitation, a more secure and settled estate for a prince to inherit would have been hard to imagine.

The life of the Duke and Duchess of York had been altered but not entirely transformed when the Duke had left the navy. He had been wholly absorbed in his career and, chafing at the enforced idleness of existence as a country gentleman, as a kind of second-in-command to his father the Prince of Wales, he sought to impose on civilian life the rigorous and simplified outlook of the Service. This involved a lifetime of self-abnegation on the part of his wife, the former Princess Mary of Teck. Born into an intellectual household which tolerated individual freedom and even eccentricity, she found herself confined: physically in the narrow surroundings of York Cottage, a dingy sub-Tudor villa, surrounded by gloomy shrubs and laurels, in the grounds of Sandringham; and emotionally among the self-sufficient children of Queen Alexandra, whose genius for affection, blunted by the extra-marital leanings of the Prince of Wales, had created an inward-looking world centred on 'darling mother-dear' which was very much the reverse of intellectual. The family group amused itself at sports, shooting and hunting; its tastes were unartistic. The Yorks' own married life was dominated by the Prince of Wales who took an obsessive interest in every detail of what went on at York Cottage. His care for his heir was doubtless fond, but the Duchess's individual enterprise and her liberal feminist outlook were stultified. Over the years she became increasingly rigid in her own ideas and came to reflect rather than reconcile her husband's obsession with punctiliousness and the minor proprieties of life.

In these dreary surroundings, overcast by the splendid paternalism of Sandringham, the Duke saw nothing wrong. When discussing the lack of domestic amenities at York

OPPOSITE Queen Victoria with her great-grand-children: Prince Edward, Princess Mary (standing) and Prince Albert (sitting) and Prince Henry in the Queen's arms. The Queen was so frail by the time this photo was taken that an attendant had to kneel behind her and support the baby's head.

OPPOSITE The Duke and Duchess of York were a formal and dignified couple who did not find it easy to relax with their children.

Cottage, he remarked amiably that he supposed the servants must sleep in the trees; and he lived contentedly there for thirty-three years, until inheritance brought Buckingham Palace, Osborne, Frogmore, Marlborough House and Balmoral, and, after the death of Queen Alexandra, Sandringham. Here, Edward, Albert, Princess Mary and, later, the three younger children grew up and absorbed or rebelled against the precepts which their parents laid down.

The old eighteenth-century Hanoverian tradition of violent disagreement between father and son had died out and there was nothing of the conflict between Edward VII and his parents in the strong bond of affection between Edward VII and his own sons. Yet the relationship between the Duke of York and his children was not an easy one. Children of the 1890s were, of course, brought up largely in the nursery, and saw their parents chiefly on rather formal and frightening afternoons. They were at the mercy of nannies, fortunate if they found a sympathetic mother-substitute like Winston Churchill's Mrs Everest, unlucky if not. In this case, at first, they were unlucky. It is remarkable to a modern generation not how the nanny regime survived, but how badly it could work. Prince Edward was adored and dominated by a head nurse who not only spoiled him but ignored Albert to the extent of feeding him in so slovenly a way that a chronic gastric weakness developed. Two years passed before she was sacked and replaced by her deputy, the much loved 'Lalla', and by then an emotional distinction between the two elder brothers had been imprinted.

The Duke of York spent a great deal of time with his children and was keen even to bathe and weigh them as babies. He gave them their first lessons in shooting, riding and fishing – and yet neither of the parents found it easy to give affection. Many years later, Queen Mary confided to Baldwin that she had never been able to sit down and chat comfortably with her children; though she qualified this to her husband's biographer, Harold Nicolson, in 1947 by saying that the difficulties had been with Edward rather than with Albert. Her husband, bluff and good-humoured with other people's children, found it hard to be tolerant of the failings of his own and tended to confuse the nursery with the wardroom. As they grew up, and became school-children and then young bachelors, he grew increasingly

18

Prince Albert with his
tutor, Mr Hansell (centre)
and Lord Desborough.

censorious, fearing perhaps a reversion to his own father's
dissolute leanings or the ribald and, in the family, legendary
exploits of George IV. The virtues he regarded most highly,
courage, manliness and discipline, he insisted on.

The result, for Prince Albert, was an excruciating shyness
in his father's presence. How far it contributed to his slow
emotional development cannot be estimated; with his elder
brother, parental strictures produced resentment and later
estrangement, for instead of encouraging them, their father
either chaffed them like errant midshipmen, or nagged as they
failed to hit the ball, grip the saddle or otherwise fulfil his
demands. Despite much happiness in childhood, these tensions
left lasting marks: Albert's stammer became a real speech defect

Edward VII and his grand-
children take the salute of
the guard of honour at
Portsmouth before sailing
out in the *Victoria and
Albert* to meet the Duke
and Duchess of York on
their return from Australia.

in his teens. Shy, nervous, easily frightened, he was content
to slip into the background, beside the mercurial Prince
Edward, and his pretty younger sister, Princess Mary.

Albert was five when Queen Victoria died in January 1901.
The Duke of York had German measles and could not attend
the funeral, so the two boys stood on that bitterly cold afternoon
to watch the kings and princes file by and bring down a symbolic
curtain on the Victorian age. The old Queen's death meant little
to them – on their visits to her they frequently cried from fright,
irritating her – but they were now translated into a new order
in which the much loved grandfather became King, and their
father Prince of Wales. Almost at once, their parents sailed to
Australia, to open the first session of the new Parliament, and

for eight months, in their absence, they tasted the delights of being spoiled at Sandringham. Lessons were abandoned for a time while Edward VII exercised his favourite '*l'art d'être grand-père*'. They received little notes signed 'ever your devoted grandpapa' and were even – and how different from York Cottage – allowed to romp in the royal presence.

Nemesis set in when the new Prince of Wales returned, for he found his elder children out of hand and concluded that the days of nursery discipline were over. Instead of nannies came Frederick Finch, who was tolerant towards them and was respected affectionately. But their education raised a more serious question. The memory of the Prince Consort's memoranda for the strict upbringing of Edward VII, and the intolerable regime laid down by Baron Stockmar, discouraged too rigid a scheme; but the choice of tutor and subjects was, unquestionably, important. The Prince of Wales had liked and respected his own tutor, the Reverend J. N. Dalton – father of a future Labour Chancellor of the Exchequer – but the qualifications of the man he actually chose, Henry Hansell, a schoolmaster already in the Royal Household, were more modest, being chiefly that he was a good yachtsman and the son of a Norfolk country gentleman. He was a bachelor and something of a bore but he had the sound conviction that boys should grow up in an environment with others of their age. When his proposal that the Princes should go to private preparatory school was vetoed, he tried to recreate, in the schoolroom at York Cottage, the atmosphere he felt they lacked; and so timetables and desks were brought in, as well as a half-hearted attempt at organised games with the village boys. These were scarcely rough and tumbles, and the nagging notes, recounting the trivia of small boys' naughtinesses, suggest both a lack of humour on the tutor's part, and a lack of sense of proportion on the part of his employer. Such reports, read after the event, incensed the Prince of Wales, who would summon his sons to the library for a dressing down.

School days were only partly relieved by the genial, burlesque figure of Monsieur Hua, the French tutor, who bore a marked resemblance to Edward VII. Albert suffered most of the two for, being slower, he was the one more often caught and, being shyer, had no answer to make during the awful sessions in the

Prince Edward and Prince Albert on the beach at Osborne Bay. They were known in the family as David and Bertie.

library. Perhaps the most sensitive, certainly the least articulate of the family, he became increasingly nervous and between the ages of seven and eight developed a pronounced stammer, the result not only of chiding and repression but of being made to write with his right hand despite a natural inclination to the left. The speech defect grew worse, through a spiral of shame and frustration, but he was given tart comments for his inaptitude at oral work, rather than sympathy. Unable to answer for himself, he became cut off from the livelier Edward and his sister Mary, to whom he had been very close. He began to acquire the look of the withdrawn child, suddenly emotional or depressed, swept by fits of anger or locked in dreams. This stress was made harder to bear by having for long periods to wear splints to cure congenital knock knees. After more than a year the treatment worked but his stammer did not improve.

23

Prince Albert with his younger brother, Prince Henry, on the banks of Loch Muick in 1907.

Albert suffered from the artificial circumstances in which princes have to pass from the nursery to manhood and mature responsibilities. It was not, of course, a wholly bleak or deprived period: there were also the country walks, riding, sports and family evenings common to any middle- or upper-class Victorian household. Seen from the outside, it was in many ways a golden age in which, despite misfortunes such as the King's appendicitis, or political drama like the great Liberal victory of 1906, the family peregrinations followed the traditional pattern, to Osborne on the Isle of Wight and up to Balmoral. Albert inherited Queen Victoria's long and deep love for Scotland, and waited impatiently for the summers when the family took the royal train north to the relative freedom of Abergeldie Castle. Around and about the River Dee, he fished, bicycled and walked, and in the landscape of the Cairngorms

24

seemed to shed the inhibitions which hampered him in more formal southern life.

Yet already there was change: the advent of a Liberal government and the crisis between Commons and Lords troubled Edward VII with great constitutional questions. He disapproved of Lloyd George and even more of the things said by Keir Hardie and the nascent Labour Party. The Prince of Wales was absent on a visit to India in 1905–6 and change was apparent even at York Cottage: Albert was becoming aware of his handicaps, a little jealous of his elder brother's facility, yet regretful when he left in 1907 to join the navy as a cadet at Osborne. He himself failed to fulfil the tutor's requirement as 'head' of the family 'school'. Lack of ability at mathematics seemed likely to debar him from the navy. But with the help of Martin David, his second tutor, and a good deal of quiet persistence, he was able to face the examining board in 1909 at the age of thirteen. They judged him the most nervous candidate they had seen, but he performed well in the written papers, scored highly in – of all things – oral French, and passed 'without hesitation'. Not for the last time, he had mastered himself and the disadvantages of being a late starter.

Until he entered the naval college for junior cadets at Osborne, Albert had led a cloistered life, remote from that of his contemporaries. Now he was flung in as an 'ordinary' cadet, to find his level among those he had not yet met, in a competitive situation and normal classes which he had never experienced. His brother had similar problems of adjustment and, years later, ended that chapter in his memoirs sardonically with a quotation from his father, 'The Navy will teach David.' Of Albert, Hansell said in his last tutorial report to the Prince of Wales: 'He is at present a scatterbrain and it is perfectly impossible to say how he will fare. . . . Like his brother he can not get on without a bit of a shove and I do hope he will not be left too much to himself. . . . The excellent discipline of Osborne will be just what he requires.' With a little warmth, he added, 'I have always found him a very straight and honourable boy, very kind hearted and generous; he is sure to be popular with other boys.'

Among seventy other thirteen-year-olds, cadet HRH Prince Albert entered the Grenville Term to find himself at the mercy of a far more rigorous discipline than he had known and a naval timetable in which everything was done at the double. His stammer and homesickness made him an easy target for bullying and he took at least a year to settle down. But he was fortunate in having as term-officer Lieutenant William Phipps, a man to whom he could look up unreservedly, a fine athlete with an eye used to discriminating between the idle and those who needed care. In the end, by perseverance, Albert charted out his own sphere where shyness did not preclude friendship. Half a dozen friends for life, with whom he could be wholly natural, dated from Osborne. At games, too, where he had a keen sense of timing, he could win applause. But in class he wavered: having reached the college by hard work rather than understanding of the matter, nothing came easily. An attack of whooping cough left him run down physically in his first year and there followed in May 1910 the death of his beloved grandfather, Edward VII. George V's elevation did not lessen his expectations; it was inconceivable to him that Prince Albert should not pass his exams to Dartmouth, the senior naval college, but, despite his repeated chidings, the Prince stayed bottom of his term.

A more quizzical spirit showed itself in Albert's response: he narrowly avoided being sent down, yet retained his composure. His tutor wrote at the time: 'With Prince Albert's mercurial temperament all things are possible.' The exams themselves, taken just before Christmas, were disastrous, leaving him sixty-eighth out of sixty-eight, and his holiday tutor, Mr Watt, had to confess to Hansell, 'I am afraid there is no disguising to you the fact that PA has gone a mucker. . . . I am afraid that their Majesties will be very disappointed.' There is no record of how son and father met that Christmas; but at least Albert had passed and was to go to Dartmouth. Glory or none, he had learned to live a normal life among other boys, no small achievement in two years.

At Dartmouth, Albert entered an institution with a century of tradition, where he was to prepare for his full naval career. Real sailing along the Devon coast and up the creeks and inlets of its harbours, held out the promise of greater independence. Of course his brother had preceded him and he still remained somewhat in the shadow, a distinction too often pointed by his

26

tutor's reports – 'It was rather like comparing an ugly duckling with a cock pheasant.' But he was again lucky in his officers, especially with Lieutenant Spencer-Cooper who encouraged him to ride, beagle and play tennis – allowing him at last to use the despised left hand. His studies were expanded with extra maths and engineering but they were frequently interrupted, by measles during the great epidemic of 1911, and by the Coronation and the spectacular review of the Fleet at Spithead. At the end of that year he touched bottom, or one from bottom, of his term.

A summer in Scotland with his holiday tutor, enlivened by shooting his first stag, offset parental criticism. Meanwhile, his growing confidence emerged in a series of quite minor and often funny escapades that led to entries in the punishment book. Skylarking was and is a part of Dartmouth experience and Albert was only typical of his generation when he helped to drive a flock of sheep into a Saturday-night dance after the lights had been cut off. The affair of the statue was, however, slightly

In 1909, at the age of thirteen, Prince Albert (seated on ground, centre) left the sheltered royal schoolroom for the boisterous companionship of the other cadets at Osborne. Prince Edward is seated third from the left.

27

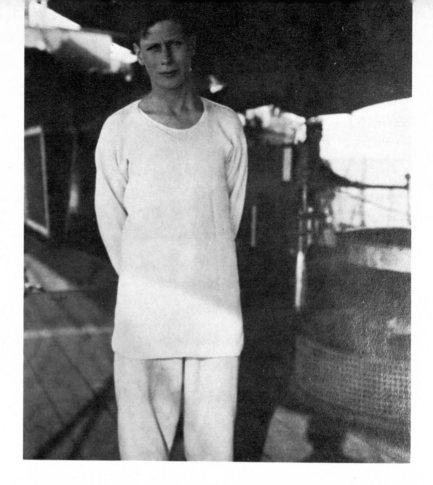

Prince Albert on board
HMS *Cumberland*, 1913.

more notorious. Inspired by the night climbers of Oxford who had set a chamber pot on top of the Martyrs' Memorial, some of the cadets determined to paint red the statue of the King which George V was due to unveil during the forthcoming royal visit. It was a matter of talk rather than action, but the extra staff who were drafted to guard the statue threatened to strike and were, according to the custom of the day, dismissed. *The Daily Graphic* printed the story in full.

The King, whose government had the miners' strike on their hands, and talk of nationalisation and workers' control to contend with, to say nothing of the troubles in Ireland and the violence of militant suffragettes at home, failed to see the joke. The visit was cancelled, and the week's holiday, ostensibly because of the strike. The real world was already breaking in. When Albert accompanied his father, during the Fleet review of 1912, out to sea in the new submarine D4, he saw that it was a symbol, like the Dreadnought, of the naval race against Germany. At sixteen he was moving rapidly towards his chosen career and the strictures were mostly past. Young for his age, still, and low on the termly list, he nevertheless appeared a sound, honest, sensible fellow and, in contrast to some of his recent ancestors, neither spoiled nor depraved. Having lived among cadets from a wide – though still restricted – social spectrum, he had acquired an easy, natural manner. (Indeed the choice of service was an indication of his father's sense of social change for, as in Germany, the navy had become the field of middle-class promotion, in contrast to the more aristocratic army regiments.)

The final stage of cadet training consisted of a tour of duty in the far seas and in January 1913 Albert joined the cruiser *Cumberland*. Confronted with hard and filthy work such as coaling, he took his share, but he proved to be a poor sailor in rough weather, a handicap which he never overcame. On another level, however, the tour was a revelation. He who had never crossed the Channel, was fêted in Tenerife and in the West Indies, and given the first taste of public enthusiasm for the symbol of monarchy and the personality of princes. In the heat of Jamaica, he was hard put to make his speeches for the excitement of the crowds and he persuaded another cadet of very similar build to stand in as decoy to do the smiling and waving at engagements where he did not have to speak. He was not afraid of people and showed himself fully appreciative of the dignity due to his status, but he did not seem to want it for himself. Another friend stood in for him and faced the avid Canadian reporters, later in the tour, while Albert wrote, repugnantly, of 'the Americans who had no manners at all and tried to take photographs all the time'. At the formal functions, the nightly balls, he was ill at ease, reluctant to ask even the prettiest Canadian girls to dance.

If he could give little of himself, he took home a vision of the colour and splendour of the West Indies and the vast energy of Canada. He had sailed up the wide St Lawrence, past Quebec and French Canada, to Montreal; he had seen the Greak Lakes and Niagara, shot the rapids and fished for salmon. On his return he looked grown up. The King was delighted and thanked Spencer-Cooper: 'I am pleased with my boy.'

Prince Albert became a midshipman in September 1913. He was never to love the *sea*, as his father had done; he had no flair

29

for yachting like his grandfather; and he never conquered sea sickness. But the service became his chosen career, and on the training ship *Collingwood*, he acquired the rudiments of a naval officer. A great deal was required of a midshipman then: to live as the lowest of the low, without privacy or privilege, to sup off bread, cheese and onions and a bottle of beer before turning in; yet, at the age of seventeen, also to exercise command. He had trained for it and he enjoyed it, as his simple factual letters show, written from ports around the Mediterranean during the manœuvres of 1914 which merged into the grand strategy of the fleet in the last year of peace.

A midshipman on board, he was a prince ashore. In Alexandria, Lord Kitchener presented the Khedive of Egypt, Abbas the Second. Albert visited the Pyramids and danced long in the British Agency. In Athens he met King Constantine of Greece and condoled with him for the assassination of his father in 1913. A straight-forward faith in the virtues of monarchy inspired a comment on an unsuccessful attempt to kill another king: 'I saw in the paper that one of those beastly anarchists tried to kill the King of Italy. What a good thing it was he who was killed by the crowd!'

In the Mediterranean, with the French and Italian fleets nearby, he could not but be aware of the tensions that crossed the diplomatic board. Back in home waters, he was caught up in the test mobilisation on 15 July, ordered by the First Lord of the Admiralty, Winston Churchill, as a warlike substitute for the usual summer manœuvres; and he was present, in his gun turret, at that climax of the old Empire when, for six hours, the Fleet passed before the King in the royal yacht at Spithead. As it sailed straight on from the test mobilisation to Scapa Flow and battle stations in the North Sea, the vaunted German High Seas Fleet, the Luxus Flotte of Tirpitz, was ranged against the new British Dreadnoughts and battle cruisers – both sides products of the naval race of the previous ten years.

George v wrote in his diary on 6 August: 'Please God it may soon be over and that he will protect dear Bertie's life.' Not since the days of William IV, who as a young man was present at the battle of Cape St Vincent, had a prince in direct line to the throne seen active service, but it was not gunfire that first endangered his life. Gastric illness, diagnosed as appendicitis,

Prince Albert was aboard
HMS *Collingwood* (left) when it sailed
past the King during the great review
of the fleet at Spithead in 1914
(below). HMS *Collingwood* is in the
foreground of the picture.

struck him at sea at the end of August and he was brought back to hospital in Aberdeen – a hazardous journey through waters mined and at risk from submarines. He missed, therefore, the action of the Heligoland Bight in which three German cruisers were sunk and the inconclusive but effective battle of the Dogger Bank which walled up the High Seas Fleet behind the German High Command's fear of losing capital ships.

Recuperating after the operation took several sad and dejected months. His friends were all at sea and the casualty lists from the Western Front were a constant reminder of the fate of his generation. While he convalesced at Sandringham, Prince Edward was posted to France as ADC to the Commander-in-Chief, Sir John French. Worse, the illness recurred in November and Sir Frederick Treves, the King's physician, advised that he should not return to sea. He was able to undertake shore duty at the Admiralty, and on the War Room maps watched the progress of the battles of the Dogger Bank and the Falkland Islands. Wistfully, he wrote: 'It is a good thing, as nobody now will be able to say that I am doing nothing.'

In 1915 he went back to duty at Scapa Flow, watching on patrol for submarines, until the gastric trouble crippled him again. He consented to go to the hospital ship, on condition that he could rejoin his own if there was a chance of action. This pledge was referred to the King: dare the Admiralty risk the Prince's life? George V had no doubt where a naval officer's duty lay, whatever the cost. But Albert fretted and did not recover. Admiral Colville, commander of the First Battle Squadron, suggested a complete change and rest at Abergeldie, yet even the Prince's favourite Highland home made little difference. At the end of 1915 he was back in the Admiralty on light duties. A visit to his brother at Divisional Headquarters gave him some insight into the ghastliness of trench warfare in Flanders: 'I saw several houses shelled by the Bosche, and the women and children running out by the back doors. That makes one think of the horrors of war – and those people are shelled every day.'

If the war was denied him, he could still act as member of the royal family. The King had been badly injured in France when his horse reared and fell on him, and so Albert was able to relieve him of such functions as opening a rifle range in the cellars of the Palace of Westminster, and entertaining, in French, the Serbian Crown Prince. Then, just in time, in May 1916, having passed his exam to Sub-Lieutenant, he returned to *Collingwood*. For eighteen months the High Seas Fleet had hugged the German coast, but in response to the stagnation of trench warfare on the Western Front, the effectiveness of the allied blockade, and the need for a victory to inspire the war effort at home, the new German Commander-in-Chief, Admiral von Scheer, adopted a more aggressive strategy. The British, under Admiral Sir John Jellicoe, had in theory planned for just such an action; but instead of proving a trap, the ambiguous battle of Jutland was claimed by both sides as a victory.

The First Battle Squadron saw most of the fighting and *Collingwood* was heavily attacked by light torpedo craft. From his action-station in A turret, Albert saw the wreck of *Invincible*, riven apart, like *Hood* twenty-four years later, by an explosion in the magazine, and the cruiser squadron decimated as they were caught by the German battleships. *Collingwood* attacked the battle-cruiser *Derfflinger*, inflicting great damage; and afterwards Albert wrote a cool, factual letter home: 'My impressions were very different to what I expected. I saw visions of the masts going over the side and funnels hurtling through the air etc. In reality, none of these things happened. No one would know to look at the ship that we had been in action. It was certainly a great experience to have been through and it shows that we are at war and that the Germans can fight if they like.'

The numerical balance sheet of Jutland was in favour of Germany, for the British lost fourteen ships including three battle cruisers, to one German battleship, four cruisers and five destroyers. But, as von Scheer reported to the Kaiser, 'It may be possible for us to inflict appreciable damage on the enemy, but there can be no doubt that even the most favourable issue of a battle on the high seas will not compel England to make peace in this war. The disadvantages of our geographical position, and the British great material superiority, cannot be compensated for by our fleet.' His reasoning led to only one conclusion: that submarine warfare must be pursued 'even at the risk of war with America'; and it was America's entry into the war which finally turned the balance against Germany.

Albert had been in no real danger, except when, as the first shots came over low, he leapt for the gun turret door, only to find it blocked by a fat petty officer, who was virtually blown in by the explosion of the second salvo. But he had learned something about himself: 'When I was on top of the turret, I never felt any fear of shells or anything else. It seems curious, that all sense of danger goes except the one longing of dealing death in every possible way to the enemy.' For three months after, there was no sickness. Then it re-doubled and Treves diagnosed a duodenal ulcer, quite possibly the long-term result of his nanny's mistreatment twenty years before. Knowledge that the cause was at last found and could if necessary be operated on, gave Albert patience through another round of shore duties, through the worst days of 1917, while the U-boats'

The German fleet sails towards the British fleet before the Battle of Jutland.

sinkings trebled in the Atlantic and the Channel. In May 1917 he went to sea for the last time, on the battleship *Malaya*, and was joined by Doctor Louis Greig, the naval surgeon, then his closest friend. The respite was temporary, and Albert at last accepted the logic not only of the operation but of an end to active service. The King's doctors debated for two months whether to agree to his wish but another attack precipitated the operation, at the end of 1917. His only regret was that the ulcer had not been found earlier, before it had become so serious.

Leaving the navy posed difficult questions. He had won esteem as a conscientious, hard-working and humane officer. To a great extent, he had thereby gained the measure of his father, who presented him with the Order of the Garter on his twenty-first birthday as a form of recognition of maturity. During his illnesses he had shown much tolerance and he was always grateful to those who bothered with him, particularly his doctors and nurses. But since he was not a permanent invalid, he could not be seen to be idle during the war and he determined to join the air force.

Victim of the prolonged rivalry of navy and army, the third service came of age only towards the end of the First World War. Even then, it needed the 1917 air raids on London before the government overcame the vested interests of the former enough to set up a unified air force. The real architects were Major General (later Air Marshal) Trenchard and Lord Cowdray, President of the Air Board, but in the political manœuvrings designed to bolster up the Coalition government, Cowdray was forced to resign. Lloyd George, sensitive to the need for Press support, appointed Lord Rothermere as Air Minister; but the air force suffered as a result. It was well enough equipped with fighters and some long-range bombers but the question of control was not settled and the disagreements erupted again when Trenchard resigned in April 1918. It was hardly surprising that, after bestowing the title Royal on the air force, George V sought to bestow prestige and stability by a closer link. So Albert joined the RNAS squadron HMS *Daedalus* at Cranwell in Lincolnshire.

Cranwell was then in embryo, almost as primitive a station as the training machines flown there, and control was uneasily

35

divided between naval and air force discipline. Albert, who took charge of the boys' squadron, found the relaxed attitude of some of the officers disturbing and he reacted by becoming something of a martinet, to the extent of reflecting on the low calibre of the petty officers around him. There was much in him of his father's and grandfather's punctiliousness about dress and drill. But he was wholly engrossed in the management of over two thousand boys and he began to learn the modern skills of flying and driving. Then came Trenchard's fall. Rothermere, too, resigned and was replaced by the Glasgow industrialist Sir William Weir. At once appeared a more professional approach to the problems of war production, but reform of the structure took a long time to filter down. Albert wrote urgently to the King: 'Everything here, as you may imagine, is in a very unsettled state, and nothing is settled yet as to what routine we are working under. We are now having a mixture of naval and military routine, which is not a success.' Unfortunately the King had little power to intervene in the political storms which wracked the government and the general staff.

In March 1918, General Ludendorff's offensive broke through the Allied lines almost to Paris. While the climactic battle raged on the Western Front, Albert's frustration at the vacillating direction of the air force, after the certainties of naval hierarchy, increased. He was transferred to the air cadet school at St Leonards in July, just as the American divisions entered the fighting and the German attack was finally turned back. Here, in more congenial surroundings, and marked out by the King's commendation for good turn-out on inspection, he warmed to the new discipline. At the very end of the war, he joined General Trenchard's staff at headquarters near Nancy and briefly experienced aerial warfare – though only from the ground.

With the signature of the Armistice came the dilemma for hundreds of thousands of servicemen. What should they do, and what sort of a world was left that they had fought to uphold? Albert did not need to worry about the most common fear, unemployment in a post-war slump; but what role was there now for a prince to fulfil? The economists and the monetary pundits recommended a return to the gold standard and the pre-war international economy. At a practical level, the Ministry of

Reconstruction, staffed with far-sighted liberals and civil servants, planned for recovery and reform; and in the election campaign, which returned Lloyd George and a huge Conservative-dominated coalition, the politicians stridently promised a land fit for heroes to live in. Meanwhile, the Labour Party dissociated itself and fought on a Socialist programme; and by groups farther to the left, the Russian Revolution was hailed as a new dawn. Marxists and Socialists joined in proposing soldiers' and workers' councils. The government entered 1919 with confused commitments, pledges, and fears of unemployment and revolution. Their state of mind can be seen from their reaction to events: the Forty Hours Strike in Glasgow ended in military occupation of the city. At Dover there were demobilisation riots, elsewhere police strikes; alarmist debates in Cabinet lasted for at least three years and found practical expression in open war in Ireland, and the spectacle of a Europe torn again and again by political and social discontent.

ABOVE LEFT A parade of the boy's wing at Cranwell, with Prince Albert in the the foreground.
ABOVE RIGHT Prince Albert on the shoulders of Louis Grieg during training at Cranwell.

2 The Search for a Career 1919-35

S UCH CERTAINTY AS THERE WAS in the post-war world belonged to Prince Edward, the elder brother. Although Prince Albert was now twenty-two and possessed of a varied and often colourful experience, he found himself virtually at a loose end. He served as the British representative during the King of the Belgians' triumphal march back into Brussels after the German army of occupation had withdrawn and he watched the emotional scene as the Belgian royal family, in their faded uniforms, signifying the struggle in exile, were received by the heroes of the resistance, Cardinal Mercier and the Burgomaster of the city. He then judged it expedient to serve out his time in France (for there had been a number of malicious slights about the length of his sick leaves in Britain during the war), and this brought about a strange encounter with the Princess Viktoria, sister of the ex-Kaiser, which indicates how completely the war had severed the old dynastic ties. She was quite unable to understand the deep hatred aroused – 'She asked after you [the King] and the family, and hoped that we shall be friends again shortly. I told her politely I did not think it was possible for a great many years!'

Indeed, a curtain had fallen between Britain and the Continent which was barely lifted for a decade. European influences, which had been so clear and close at Queen Victoria's Court and in the wider cultural and social environment of Britain in the 1890s and 1900s, had been disrupted and were not to be reawakened in Prince Albert's lifetime. During the inter-war years, Britain became isolated, even anti-European, a phenomenon evident at many levels, from diplomacy to the decline in the number of people taking holidays abroad. Crude nationalism was enhanced by the vindictive emotions of a dozen war-weary countries, while at the Peace Conference in Paris the allied leaders, President Wilson, Lloyd George, Clemenceau and Orlando sat down to redraw the map of Europe, returning to France Alsace and Lorraine, and creating out of the shattered fragments of the Austro-Hungarian Empire, ambitious national states such as Czechoslovakia.

Prince Albert decided to learn to fly in earnest. If this was to be his future, then he could no longer remain a 'quirk' or land-based officer. After several weeks' training in France, the King allowed him to return and early in 1919 he joined the Air

Ministry staff and started flying lessons at Croydon. With Louis Greig, who took instruction at the same time, he earned his wings and became the first qualified pilot in the royal family. But his doctors forbade him to fly solo, and even during the test he was accompanied by his instructor, Lieutenant Coryton.

As with many of the things he schooled himself to do, Albert never really enjoyed flying, and the air force offered him only a temporary billet. He was determined to find a career both useful and congenial – yet while he dissociated himself from the ornamental existence typical of so many nineteenth-century royalty, he was not in a position to benefit from the freedom of his generation. He was never identified with the roisterous style of living of the 'gay young things' of the twenties, amiably caricatured in Evelyn Waugh's *Vile Bodies*, which captured the society headlines and the flash bulbs, and which was bitterly resented by the political left and Non-conformist morality; nor was he egalitarian and emancipated. Conscious enough, from his father's homilies, of the dangers of idleness and substantial

Prince Edward and Prince Albert in France during the war.

wealth, he aspired to something more than the round of secondary state functions. But his father, who had been given insight into state affairs by Edward VII, would not or could not delegate responsibility.

The concept of monarchy was not attacked in Britain after the war as it was in Germany, Austria and Holland, and later in Italy and Spain, but it was not free from questioning. The wealth and social position of the royal family represented a particular affront to the Labour Party. Newly wedded to the 1918 Constitution with its clear Socialist aims, the Labour Party pledged itself at home to nationalisation of the major industries and to collective security abroad, and although it did not become the official Opposition till 1922, its size clearly foreshadowed a new alignment of British parliamentary politics. Lloyd George's policy of prolonging the Coalition appeared likely to destroy the old Liberal and Conservative parties and perhaps precipitate a Labour government, a development which George V viewed with despondency. Just before the Armistice, Lord Cromer had written: 'In spite of the increasing labours and devotion to public duties of the King and Queen during the last three years, the fact remains that the position of the monarchy is not so stable now, in 1918, as it was at the beginning of the war.' Despite his lack of sympathy for the modern world, George V did succeed in finding an answer, as his friendships with Labour leaders and his robust commonsense advice during the industrial unrest of the 1920s showed; but it was not one in which he judged his sons capable of participating. He planned their lives, yet he was rarely satisfied with the outcome.

The first exercise the King judged appropriate for his second son was to go to Trinity College, Cambridge to readjust to civilian life and to complete his formal education. He saw, accurately enough, that in a growing climate of anti-war opinion, with a huge public investment of hope in disarmament and the League of Nations, the Services were not likely to offer the career which he had himself known in the 1890s. Hence Albert, decorously obedient, went up, like his grandfather, 'to learn everything that will be useful for the time to come'. There were no echoes of Edward VII's lively behaviour, however, in his modest life in Trumpington, where Greig was his

Prince Albert receiving
an honorary degree at
Cambridge in 1922.

equerry. Unfortunately, besides giving instructions for him to
live out of college, ostensibly for his greater freedom, the King
deemed only one year of study necessary. It was a mistake;
Albert was isolated, being away from the main undergraduate
stream, and made no lasting friends.

On the other hand, he learned much from his brilliant tutors,
the historian J. R. M. Butler, son of a former Master of Trinity,
and the economist Dennis Robertson. Both were able to
enliven the dullest courses; which may have been necessary
because the Prince's studies in history, economics and civics
were bound heavily by sombre authorities such as Dicey's
Law of the Constitution. Sober, uncritical by undergraduate
standards, Albert stored away the precepts and principles of
Dicey and Bagehot, even though he scarcely conceived that
he might one day be king himself.

One year was too short a time to do more than sample the
rich variety of Cambridge life. Although he joined the undergraduate clubs, punted on the Cam and drove his motorbike
around the countryside, even that year was interrupted by state
occasions. He had to entertain the Shah of Persia and the re-
barbative French President, Raymond Poincaré, and he had to
face the constant embarrassment of his stammer, a defect which
could not be overcome by effort alone. Despite courses of

A miniature of
Lady Elizabeth Bowes-
Lyon, who married
Prince Albert, Duke of
York, in April 1923.

treatment by experts in speech therapy, public performances
were anathema to him. His only way out was to speak extempore but, for decorum's sake, this was rarely allowed. His
letters record dismal anxiety: 'That dreadful speech [at a
Royal Academy dinner]. I hope it will go off alright, though it
is something of an ordeal to go through.'

At the end of the Easter term in 1920 he went down, gazetted already in the Birthday Honours as Duke of York. The accolade brought a touching exchange of gratitude between father and son, rare enough over the next few years because the King continued to exercise his tetchy authority despite the fact that his older sons were now well on in their twenties. At times, not unreasonably, they rebelled. In many ways, it was easier for the Prince of Wales, who spent much of these years abroad, than for the new Duke of York who actually lived in his father's house. Hence perhaps the survival of sudden fits of temper, followed by nervous exhaustion, the signs not of a quarrelsome temperament but of repression.

Among the routine offices of a member of the royal family, which occupied the Duke in the next decade, one thing stood out. He found a cure for his stammer. Despite the constant encouragement of his wife after his marriage in 1921, he had begun to despair. Typically, as President of the British Empire Exhibition in 1925, he had felt excruciating tension at the thought of making a speech in Wembley Stadium, where the Prince of Wales had performed admirably a year before. 'Bertie got through alright but there were some rather long pauses', the King, who was present, wrote drily. The search for a cure lasted nearly ten years, until the Duke was thirty, when he was persuaded to see one last expert, Lionel Logue, an Australian therapist who had had great success persuading sufferers that they were neither different from others nor mentally retarded. When the Duke walked through the door of his consulting room, Logue saw 'a slim quiet man, with tired eyes and all the outward symptoms of the man upon whom habitual speech defect had begun to set the sign'. Steadily he taught him not only the techniques of breathing rhythm but that it was *his* responsibility to carry out the discipline. By the end of 1926, the Duke was better; not cured, for when tired or anxious, the defect caught up again, but on the way to control. For the first time in his life he was able to talk on equal terms with the King, despite the latter's increasing deafness. Nevertheless, the stammer held him back in the early 1920s from many of the more exciting royal duties.

In 1922 the Duke represented the King as 'Koom' or chief sponsor at the wedding of the daughter of Queen Marie of Romania to the King of the Serbs, and in that Balkan cockpit

45

George v and his four sons
riding in Windsor Park.
Even when the Princes
became adults, they never
lost their awe of him.

he made an effective ambassador. But when he asked if he could follow the Prince of Wales and visit the Empire, in the wake of the critically important Dominion Prime Ministers' Conference of 1923, the King demurred, making the excuse that the Duke had only just married and needed time to settle down.

It was not an excuse that held good in October 1923, when the Duke became of real service to the state. Another Balkan invitation had arrived, asking him to stand as godfather to the son of King Alexander of Yugoslavia and as 'Koom' at Prince Paul's wedding, but at the time the Duke had no taste for it. Then, following the murder by bandits of an Italian boundary commission in Greece, Mussolini ordered an attack on the Greek island of Corfu. A European crisis blew up and embroiled both the League of Nations and the Ambassadors' Conference in Paris. For a moment there was a danger that France might side with Italy against Greece. The British took a strong line and insisted on the competence of the League to settle disputes; but Mussolini evaded protest and won a grossly partial judgment from the Ambassadors' Conference, to the financial loss of Greece and the lasting detriment of the League. Afterwards, Baldwin and Curzon, the Prime Minister and Foreign Secretary, felt it necessary to show that Britain was not uninterested

46

in Greek security. The Foreign Office asked the Duke to change his mind.

Somewhat surprised at the speed of events, the Duke and Duchess agreed, and acquitted themselves admirably in what was obviously a diplomatic gesture of support. Whether the Duke was aware of the implications of his visit or the web of dynastic ties woven by Queen Marie of Romania is doubtful: his letters showed nothing of them but reflected chiefly his pleasure at being able to show off his bride to his Balkan cousins and wonder at the magnificence of Orthodox Church ceremonial, mixed with occasional absurdity, as when the aged Patriarch actually dropped the baby in the font.

The political significance of royal visits showed more starkly when the Yorks arrived in Northern Ireland in 1924. Only three years before, the King had opened the Northern Ireland Parliament with a memorable speech which charted the way towards a truce in the south and the Treaty of 1921. Since then, the north, led by Sir James Craig, had toyed briefly with negotiations with Eire but, then, alienated by the civil war in the south, had withdrawn into an entrenched Protestant-dominated position. The manner of the Duke's visit, his acceptance of the freedom of Londonderry and Belfast and an honorary degree from Queens' University, was designed to show that the north had not been forgotten, that Stormont was the equal of the Dail. It was not judged an opportune time to remind Irishmen that the Act of 1921 had provided for an overall Council of Ireland. The Unionists put on a splendidly patriotic show, and dutifully – and a little naïvely – the Duke made no distinction between his reception in the different religious quarters of Belfast. 'We were received in the same wonderful way wherever we went, even in the poorest parts, which shows how very loyal they all are to you', he told the King.

Finally, in 1925, he was allowed out to East Africa, though the visit was more a holiday than a state occasion. He was captivated by Africa from the moment of their arrival. On the coast they were engulfed by the colourful blend of Arab, Swahili and Portuguese civilisations; inland lay the plains, teeming with big game of every variety, and the mountain ranges of the Aberdares and Mount Kenya. Massed tribesmen danced for the royal couple, who varied their time between watching game and exercising their skill at shooting. Excitement abounded: the Duke stumbled on a rhinoceros in the bush and the cameramen who pursued him claimed that he had been charged. He carried away a confusion of bright images, of forest and rolling plains, and of the Nile down which they sailed to Khartoum, but what chiefly impressed him were the visions of the Governor, Sir Robert Coryndon, Cecil Rhodes's former private secretary and an imperialist of Lord Milner's stamp. Kenya and Uganda were then, for white settlers, only a generation old. They had just been saved from the Germans in the war: afterwards, Tanganyika Protectorate had been added to British colonial territory. To the Duke, vast possibilities opened up. He had noted: 'There is a very good type of settler out here and most of them are gentlemen in the true sense of the word'; later he wrote to Queen Mary: 'Everything is so new and utterly different to other parts of the Empire. Being so young it should be made gradually by the best people we can produce from home.'

In the mid 1920s, however, the imperial ideal succumbed to different changes. The war had developed the distinct economies and political sensibilities of the Dominions, who had already proved mature enough to dissociate themselves from Lloyd George's aggressive policy in 1922, when the Chanak incident nearly brought Britain to war with Turkey. The last chance of forming a coherent economic and defensive Dominion network – a pale reflection of Joseph Chamberlain's tariff policy of 1903 – vanished when Baldwin failed to carry the British General Election of 1923. Afterwards, bereft of quota and tariff agreements, the Dominions continued to develop along their own divergent paths. Britain was left primarily responsible for imperial defence, a liability which in the 1930s became a crippling constraint on her foreign policy; Canada drifted inevitably into the economic orbit of the United States; Australia and New Zealand began to look with increasing unease at the commercial and military growth of Japan; while in South Africa the deep divisions between English and Afrikaner hardened in spite of the skill of Field Marshal Smuts and General Hertzog in balancing their claims. In India, the only non-white Dominion, political unrest and communal disorder swelled together, always too fast for the ruling power to contain.

48

Differing interests imposed great strains as the old ideals of Empire were slowly transformed into the new concept of Commonwealth. The strength of Dominion links often lay in their imprecision and no formula could paper over the fact that Britain's European policy, especially the Locarno Pact, guaranteeing the western frontier of Germany, ran counter to what the Dominions wished Britain to do for them. For these reasons, George v was careful to emphasise the practical and symbolic importance of the monarch as head of the Commonwealth. He interested himself closely in the appointment of Governors General and he used the Prince of Wales as a royal ambassador frequently in the 1920s. The ecstatic receptions given on these tours seemed to confirm that importance, just as the debates over the Irish Treaty of 1921 and de Valera's claim for 'external association' reflected keen concern for the form of the oath of allegiance to the Crown. Nevertheless, the creation of a stable relationship needed new formalities and after the 1926 Dominion Prime Ministers' Conference, A.J. Balfour was appointed chairman of the constitutional committee whose report led finally, in 1931, to the Statute of Westminster, and an end to the powers of the Crown over Dominion legislation.

Six months after Balfour began his deliberations, the Duke of York sailed for Australia and New Zealand to open the new Parliament building in Canberra. Freed largely from his stammer, which had at first deterred Stanley Bruce, the Australian Prime Minister, from inviting him, the Duke faced up to the demands of a full royal tour, infinitely more exacting than his experiences in East Africa, and conducted all the time in the fullest blaze of publicity. Two speeches in the morning, a luncheon, a garden party and a dinner in the evening was by no means an unusually heavy day, and how great a part the Duchess played in his support could be seen when she fell ill with tonsillitis during the tour of New Zealand, leaving him scarcely able to continue alone.

Their charm and total lack of pomposity was essential to win an ovation in Australia where, in contrast to the inbuilt veneration for monarchy shown in New Zealand, they had to earn the cheers as personalities not symbols, and against a natural inclination to flaunt egalitarian independence. During the

The Duchess's charm was a great asset to the Duke, particularly in his overseas tours. Here they are greeted at Las Palmas on their way to Australia.

hectic and exhausting round of receptions and duties from one state to another, over two whole months, they succeeded. The Duke was hailed as a sportsman, for his skills at tennis, riding and fishing; and the Duchess evinced that spontaneous glow of affection which was to clothe her in public and in private in the future.

'A really genuine young man, with decided opinions of his own, and that is what we like', proved to be a typical comment. The Duke was deeply moved by the spirit of loyalty, and he made Anzac Day, the eleventh anniversay of the bloody landings in Gallipoli, in many ways the most solemn moment of the visit. 'Let us try to live more worthily of those who made the great sacrifice for us', he said, with a feeling born of his own experience, 'and to do the utmost that lies in our power to maintain and hand down to the children who come after us those traditions of loyalty, fortitude and duty which animated those gallant men, and on the preservation of which the whole welfare and security of the Empire depend.' Such words, perfectly attuned to the feelings of Australian veterans, ensured respect. Later, on the steps of the new Parliament building in

The Duchess meets some aborigines during the tour of Australia.

Canberra, and before the formal speech from the throne, he broadcast to the Australian people and conveyed, in surroundings so new that they looked like a film set, that sense of continuity over time from which the Commonwealth link was to be made.

'I have so much more confidence in myself now', he wrote to the King. Appreciative voices reported him; among them Sir Tom Bridges, Governor of South Australia: 'The visit has done untold good and has certainly put back the clock of dissension and disloyalty twenty-five years so far as this State is concerned.' On his return, the Duke expressed his feelings at a Guildhall banquet: 'I return a thorough optimist. When one has travelled over the vast extent of the Empire, when one has witnessed what our fathers have accomplished, when one has seen how the great and creative purpose of our kinsmen have triumphed over the most tremendous difficulties, it is impossible to despair of the future of the British race.'

But the King, whose constant advice had varied from kindly hints to rather niggling criticism of dress and ceremonial, failed to show appreciation; and rejected, as he had done with the Prince of Wales, the Duke's request to have access to the reports of Governors General and Dominion Prime Ministers, or to become acquainted with foreign statesmen. Only with great reluctance did he permit him to see a carefully screened selection of Foreign and Dominions Offices papers, even after an illness in November 1928, so serious that the Prince of Wales was recalled from East Africa. Worse, there were no more royal tours. Apart from attendance at royal funerals in Europe, indeed, the Duke was scarcely called abroad. In 1930, his name was suggested as a possible candidate for Governor General of Canada, but it was vetoed by the Dominions Secretary, J. H. Thomas, on the curious ground that Canada, being contiguous with the United States, needed a more democratic figure. It is more likely that the intention was to spare the royal family involvement in the increasing bitterness shown by French Canadians and the isolationism so evident at the Imperial Economic Conference, held at Ottawa in 1932.

Only one other duty of state occupied the Duke before 1936. It was entirely appropriate that, as the first since Queen Victoria fully to appreciate his Scottish inheritance, he should represent the King as Lord High Commissioner to the General Assembly of the Church of Scotland in 1929. The occasion itself was of unusually profound significance. After nearly a century, the Free Church, which had seceded in 1843, was to be reunited with the Church of Scotland. The Duke took his place as the meeting-point between Church and State, between the Moderators, who had asked for this first royal appointment since 1679, and the government in London. Later, in October 1929, he returned (because of his father's recurrent illness) to witness the final reconciliation and healing of the schism, as the two Moderators shook hands before a crowd of a hundred thousand people. The religious ceremony evoked the Duke's own faith and seemed to identify him particularly with Scotland, her culture and her people.

During the fifteen years after Cambridge, the Duke of York showed himself peculiarly sensitive to the social stresses set up in the world of industry at a time of unemployment and stagnation. It was not a sphere in which the royal family had taken great interest, apart from the obvious encounters such as opening new factories or launching ships, since the days of the Prince Consort, whose close interest in manufacturing processes had found its most vivid expression in the Great Exhibition of 1851. Industrial matters scarcely penetrated Queen Victoria's widowed seclusion; Edward VII, though friendly with many business magnates, concerned himself scarcely at all with the source of their wealth. George V, though preoccupied with the ideological clashes between capital and organised labour, did not find it necessary to investigate on the shop floor.

Yet the 1920s witnessed the most prolonged and widespread industrial discontent in Britain's history. Even before the 1914 war, industrialists had been slow to modernise the staple industries, and even slower to branch out into electricity and chemicals. Widespread fears about the pattern of investment were not allayed by any government direction and for ten years the relations between employers and employed deteriorated, punctuated after 1910 by massive strikes. During the war, the vigour of the older industries of coalmining, heavy engineering, shipbuilding and cotton was artificially stimulated by the demands of war production, only to be cut short by the slump after 1920. For the following two decades, they were cursed with falling demand, loss of markets and excess capacity in outdated machinery and, above all, in manpower. Thus, while the later 1920s saw a boom in newer industries, the black cloud of over a million unemployed settled on the once prosperous areas of old industrial Britain.

Caught by loss of profits and markets, many manufacturers sought to lower wages; and whereas the miners struck in 1921 to gain higher wages, later action, above all the General Strike of 1926, was primarily defensive. Hence the bitterness and the violence of despair, and the mistrust shown by unions who believed that the government was hand in glove with employers' associations. Successive attempts to break through towards a policy of industrial conciliation proved unsuccessful until, in the exhausted aftermath of the General Strike, the Mond-Turner talks led to a tacit understanding between the two sides that lasted into the 1930s.

Almost alone among industrial nations, Britain suffered ten years of large-scale unemployment before the world depression

53

began. Preoccupied with the threat of class conflict, governments feared subversion, Communists and foreign extremists. On the whole, they were without much justification. George v feared republican outcry, yet found even the Irish susceptible to his intervention in Belfast in 1921. The Labour Cabinet debated whether or not to carry top hats when kissing hands in 1924 but only the Communist Party made an issue of abolishing kingship. The second fear, however, was far more real. How could the authority of either King or Government be used to renew the political compact with the dispossessed and the unemployed and prevent, not so much revolution, as alienation of the working class? In particular, 'The monarchy and its cost', as Lord Esher had seen in 1918, 'will have to be justified in the eyes of a war-worn and hungry proletariat, endowed with a huge preponderance of voting power.'

It turned out to be easier to thank the Dominions for their war-effort than to acknowledge the debt to the people of Britain. In November 1918 a massive crowd of ex-servicemen, during a march past in Hyde Park, had unfurled banners in front of the King himself, protesting grievances which he barely understood. The gulf between palace and shop floor appeared unbridgeable. But the Duke of York had some experience of working men. As a midshipman he had not been vastly distant from the lower deck and he had supervised hundreds of boy cadets. He had also a conscience that the treatment meted out to the veterans, whether of the trenches or of the wartime factories, was squalid and inadequate.

In the early days of the war, the gross exploitation of migrant workers, particularly of women in the munitions industry, had brought together Lloyd George and Seebohm Rowntree in setting up a welfare department in the Ministry of Munitions. To cope with the problems of the influx of unskilled female workers, of broken families, rising rents and illegitimacy, Rowntree drafted the Reverend Robert Hyde, chairman of the Maurice Hostel settlement and a specialist in work among young people. At the end of the war, when a parsimonious Treasury replaced the unofficial experts by Home Office civil servants, Hyde continued his work in a private capacity, but soon ran into trouble, with the unions who saw his boys' welfare organisation as a counter to collective bargaining, and

54

with employers who considered it to be tinged with Socialism. Supported, however, by an all-party group, which included R.H.Tawney, J.H.Thomas, George Lansbury and Bishop Gore, he looked for a royal sponsor. The Archbishop of Canterbury, Randall Davidson, was on the point of setting up his commission on Christianity and Industrial Problems and, *via* his chaplain, the message reached the Duke of York, who agreed enthusiastically, 'providing there's no damned red carpet about it'.

Hyde had envisaged his organisation as a form of social cement, carefully grouted into the cracks, 'checking and guiding aright those tendencies which we all deplore'. But the Duke made more of it than a form of paternalism: when he visited a

PUNCH, OR THE LONDON CHARIVARI.—FEBRUARY 6, 1924.

THE LABOURS OF MACHERCULES.

The problems facing the first Labour prime minister, Ramsay MacDonald.

factory, he did so in working hours; he asked questions and he expected answers which might lead to action. He inspected the work of individuals, remembered their faces – often for years – and hoped, in so far as it was possible, to see the shop floor as it really was. He climbed scaffolding, went down mines, grew accustomed to a safety helmet, made himself stomach the stench of a glue factory or the noise of blasting. When Queen Mary suggested that he extend his scope, the organisation was rechristened the Industrial Welfare Society and he became its first president.

The Prince Consort's interest in industry had been intellectual rather than practical. The Duke, in contrast, sought physical acquaintance with working-class conditions of life, and although he could never identify with them, he made efforts which were genuinely welcomed. He was not often put off by bland answers from managers, and one wrote: 'Of all the visitors we had here, I never met one who asked more sensible questions or showed greater understanding of our fundamental problems. He does like getting to the bottom of things.' Even if he appeared powerless to effect change, his visits to over a hundred and fifty factories between 1920 and 1935 had practical results. Conditions, after all, were in many cases no better than before 1914. If the Duke was to inspect a coalmine, then the

The Duke and Duchess of York about to descend the Glamis pit at Kibblesworth Colliery, Durham.

management might well decide to install pithead baths; if a cotton mill, then the safety precautions which an over-worked inspectorate was hard-put to enforce.

The Duke believed, quite simply, that if royalty showed no interest, then it had no answer to republicanism. In 1920 he told the Society, 'There is a new industrial philosophy abroad with which we must identify ourselves and of which we must be pioneers.' The fulsome Press, of course, dubbed him 'the Industrial Prince', and the *Daily Worker* derided him for mere paternalism. George v called industrial relations 'my second son's department'. Some of his activities, such as the golf match on a Welsh miners' course between the Duke, his Comptroller, the miners' leader Frank Hodges and Evan Williams, head of the Mine Owners' Association – protagonists of the 1921 strike – had a theatrical effect, like the famous football match at Plymouth between strikers and policemen during the General Strike; but, if slightly unreal, they at least reflected a non-violent approach to potentially violent disputes.

After 1927, the pressures eased. Employers began to look elsewhere for economies, *via* combines, mechanisation and, catch-word of the period, 'rationalisation'. Most unions, weakened by loss of members, accepted the 'peace in industry' olive branch, and the Baldwin government turned busily to schemes of manpower transference and the derating of industry. Unemployment, however, rose rapidly to a peak of three millions in 1932 and fell only slowly afterwards. The depressed areas spiralled downwards into a pit of misery and poverty beyond the wit or ability of government to prevent. In sharp contrast, the south and the Midlands prospered, disturbed only by the hunger marches and the rare newspaper investigations into the other England of the dole queue.

The work of the Industrial Welfare Society became entirely acceptable at a time when the relief of unemployment underlay most political debates. The Duke of York's philosophy was scarcely revolutionary and perhaps amounted to no more than 'acknowledging that indefinable element we have always described as the human factor'. Unlike the Prince of Wales, whose emotional response to the plight of poverty-stricken families tended to promise more than politicians could fulfil, he confined himself to the limits where enlightened awareness could produce results. Pensions funds, promotion schemes, health and sickness benefits, sports facilities, were the tasks he set employers – because he rarely chided workmen, believing that there were few bad ratings, only obtuse officers. These goals supplemented the creation of a welfare state. Yet he never shirked the moral challenge of Socialism and was at least a little influenced by ideas going back to William Morris. In his last address to the IWS in 1935, he said: 'I feel there is a change of spirit abroad, recreating many of the best features of working life in the Middle Ages, a spirit which, to a large extent, was lost in the development of the factory system. We must prove that throughout history there has always been an impetus to make a society in which men are able to work together in harmony.'

Although the Industrial Welfare Society offered a special field for his talents, the Duke also looked for a more personal involvement. He believed that the gulf between working and upper class was the greatest threat to the fabric of society but that, given an early enough start in life, it could be bridged. In 1921 he attended a football match between boys from Briton Ferry Steelworks and Westminster School and afterwards was inspired by the organiser, the millionaire philanthropist and biscuit manufacturer Sir Alexander Grant, to reflect on the possibility of a meeting ground where boys could talk as well as play. Many pitfalls opened up, however, because while football offered common rules and aims, could there be any more permanent institution free of artifice and embarrassment, or worse?

The Duke thought of an answer, compounded of Boy Scout traditions, the popular 'back to the land' movement – and the experience of the Industrial Welfare Society. He would himself play host at a camp like Cranwell without military discipline. An appeal to industry was launched; Sir Alexander funded the first camp (and part of many others) and Commander Coote was appointed as chief organiser. A wartime aerodrome at New Romsey in Kent, close to the sea and with adequate buildings, offered an excellent site.

The scheme stood or fell by the success of the mixture. The Duke had hoped that a hundred public schools and a hundred firms would each send two boys, aged seventeen to nineteen,

The Duke at one of his
boys' camps, 1936.

for a week. But would they come, even under the umbrella
of royal patronage? On the first occasion, lacking clear instructions, some of the public schoolboys turned up dressed for
the City. Both sides were stiff and chilly on the journey down.
But the staff persevered, as if this had been expected. Once in
camp kit, identical shirts and shorts, some of the distinctions
vanished; competitive games, organised in sections of twenty
carefully mixed boys, did the rest. Shrewdly, the Duke had
advised against any game known only to one group, so new
ones were thought up. After three days, despite some cynical
comment in the Press, he arrived to take his part as host, and
chanced his prestige on the camp's success. Of that there was
no question. Year after year it was to continue, improved by
experience, never again lacking recruits. The Duke changed
the style of his annual visits, later spending a whole day playing
games and swimming with the boys, though his advisers would
not let him wander, as he wished, incognito among his guests.
A pleasant tradition grew up that men prominent in public
life should be invited down, dined and then given precisely

The Duchess of York was the second youngest child of the Earl and Countess of Strathmore. In this picture she is standing to the right of her mother, surrounded by her father, brothers and sisters.

three minutes to make a complicated speech, with a blank cartridge to cut them short at the end.

For his own, personal event, the Duke craved privacy, so he transferred the camp in 1930 from Romsey, where it was too close to day-trippers and cameramen, to Southwold in Suffolk. As King, in 1939, he finally ended what he had created, by taking a select group of only two hundred up to Abergeldie Castle, his childhood retreat, where he played the role of camp chief himself. Every day that week he out-walked the boys in the hills, or gave them tea and supper at Balmoral with the Queen and the two Princesses. Extending to them his knowledge and love of the countryside, only weeks before the Second World War, made him completely happy. The shy, retiring Prince Albert could hardly have carried this off fifteen years before; nor could the boys have rallied to him if he had not been able to radiate sympathy and understanding. The idea of the camp is hard to describe to a more cynical age, but it was best put by a Cabinet visitor in the 1920s: 'What did distinguish it was the real and vital spiritual force which animated alike the organisers and the camp – the vital force of help, of co-operation – in one word, of love.'

As a young bachelor, the Duke of York found Buckingham Palace an uncongenial home. His father's nagging, well-meant though it was, chafed him as much as his own affection for his parents seemed unrequited. But in 1920, at one of the many small private dances of the season, he met Lady Elizabeth Bowes-Lyon, and he saw her again in the autumn of 1921. She was the ninth child of the Earl and Countess of Strathmore, an ancient Scottish family, whose youth had been spent either at their Hertfordshire house, St Paul's Waldon Bury, or at the castle of Glamis, rich in historical association dating back to the time of Macbeth. She was a light of the London season, a scintillating dancer, full of grace and sparkle. The Duke shyly allowed his affection to appear in his letters to his mother but scarcely dared speak of it to the lady herself.

In her family circle, he found himself wholly at ease, but he doubted if she would ever give up the richness and freedom of life in a great aristocratic household for the constraints and stifling publicity of a royal marriage. Deeply troubled, he sought the advice of an old friend and experienced politician, J. C. C. Davidson, on the occasion of a visit to dedicate the war

Queen Mary with the Duke and Duchess of York at Balmoral. Both the King and Queen had a high regard and affection for their first daughter-in-law.

The wedding ceremony in Westminster Abbey, April 1923.

memorial at Dunkirk, in 1922. Davidson replied that he must not give up, and that his own wife had refused him several times before finally saying yes.

To this he replied that his case was different from mine. The King's son cannot propose to the girl he loves, since custom requires that he must not place himself in the position of being refused, and to that ancient custom the King his father firmly adhered. Worse still, I gathered that an emissary had already been sent to ascertain whether the girl was prepared to marry him, and that it had failed.

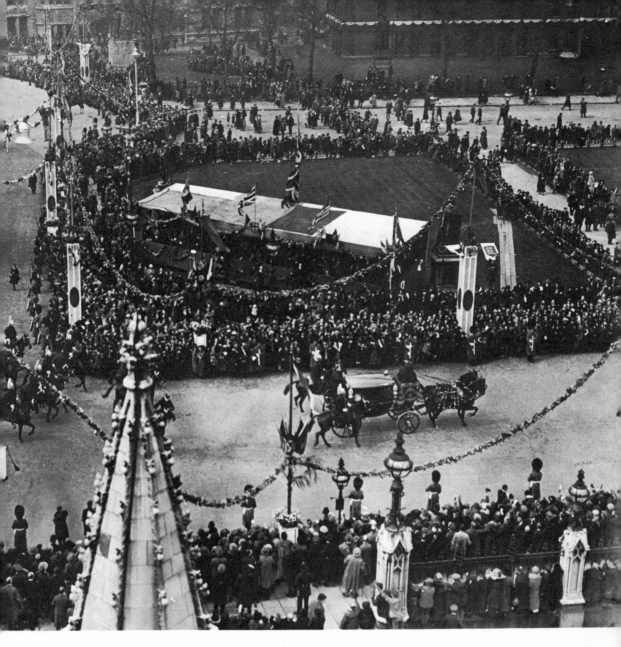

The question was, what was he to do? He could not live without her, and certainly he would never marry anyone else.

The advice that I ventured to give him was simple. I suggested that in the year of grace 1922 no high spirited girl of character was likely to accept a proposal made at second hand; if she was as fond of him as he thought she was, he must propose to her himself. . . . His mood when we parted was much brighter and more buoyant than at the beginning of our talk.

Shortly afterwards, he was able to announce his engagement

The bridal coach leaving the abbey.

63

to the King and Queen, who gladly consented. 'Elizabeth is charming, so pretty and engaging and natural. Bertie is supremely happy', Queen Mary wrote, after meeting her; the King, too, was outspokenly enthusiastic at his son's choice. The marriage took place with the utmost splendour in Westminster Abbey in April 1923, and although an obscurantist Chapter refused the newly-chartered BBC permission to broadcast the service, the procession offered the country a pageant in the grey days following the collapse of Lloyd George's Coalition government. Among all the fairy tale atmosphere of the gossip columns, two comments stood out: *The Times* commendation of the Duke – 'Young as he is, he has known enough of frustration to make all admirers of pluck and perseverance the more anxious to wish him happiness and success in the venture'; and the same paper's mordant comment that his elder brother was still unwed. But the ecstasy was reserved for the new Duchess, both then and later, and the Duke was content that it should be so.

George V sent a valediction, unchaining a little his reserve of affection, now that his son was to be head of a family in his own house. He wished him as great happiness as he had had in married life and the wish was granted many times over, for the Duke found not only love and joy but support from his partner, an end to his melancholic introspection, a vision of the brighter side of his duty in life. She eased his stammer, calmed his anger and helped to create a family sympathy which reflected the natural warmth of her own upbringing. In that supportive atmosphere, he was truly reborn and never failed to acknowledge the debt.

After a honeymoon in Scotland, they moved into White Lodge, a former hunting-box in Richmond Park. It had been Queen Mary's earliest home, and it reflected her taste because she decorated it for them, just as York Cottage had been done up for her by Queen Alexandra. It soon became a burden, being large, expensive to run and far too exposed to the public in the park. The Duchess, unwilling to abandon society at the age of twenty-three, pined for something in central London but not until 1927 were they able to find what they wanted. There were household problems, too. Louis Greig had been an invaluable guide and philosopher as well as friend. He had taught the Duke

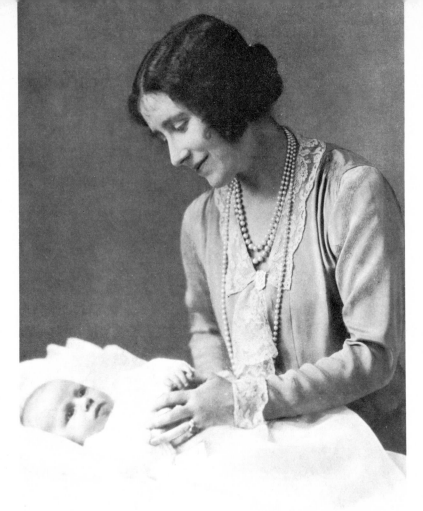

The Duchess of York with
her second daughter,
Princess Margaret Rose.

and, as he said, 'put steel into him', providing in his own family
circle an alternative to the austerity of Buckingham Palace. His
devotion was total, even in little things such as giving up a
chance of winning the RAF singles tennis championship in 1920,
in order to partner the Duke and win the doubles. But while
he remained a friend, new appointments were needed. A
number of self-effacing equerries and Comptrollers followed,
but none took his place.

The Yorks borrowed Chesterfield House until they found a
London house of their own, 145 Piccadilly, and dance succeeded
dance, as the great political families vied for the glittering prizes
of the season, or as they themselves entertained, more modestly
but no less gaily. Their first child was born just before the
General Strike, on 21 April 1926 and christened Elizabeth

65

The Royal Lodge,
Windsor, was the private
home of the York family.

Alexandra Mary. 'Elizabeth of York sounds so nice', the King
wrote appreciatively. No one mentioned Victoria either then
or in August 1930 when the second daughter, Margaret Rose,
was born at Glamis. (On that occasion the unfortunate Home
Secretary, Clynes, duty bound to attend all royal births, from
excessive zeal or misinformation arrived in Scotland a fortnight
early and had to find lodgings at Airlie Castle nearby.)

The public affection lavished on the two Princesses may be
gauged not only from the sentimental slush put out by the mass
circulation dailies but from the warmth of the staid Moderator
of the Church of Scotland who unbent so far at the General
Assembly as to speak of 'our dear Princess'. As time passed,
the assumption that Elizabeth might one day be Queen, grew,
though the Prince of Wales, who remained unmarried, was not
forty until 1934.

A chill wind blew through the great houses after the 1929
slump. Two years later, just before the formation of the
National Government, the Yorks moved into Royal Lodge,
Windsor Park, George IV's country retreat, designed by Wyatt-

ville but never finished and half demolished after his death. In the general demand for retrenchment and an end to conspicuous spending, which led the King to give up shooting in Windsor Park and sacrifice £50,000 from the Civil List, the Duke of York sadly auctioned his horses and abandoned hunting. But with the dawn of recovery in 1932–3, he followed the pattern of that large section of the public which aspired to property ownership and consumer goods, and began to restore the dilapidated Lodge. Wyattville's magnificent unfinished salon became the centrepiece and, with two added wings, formed an ideal family house. The Duke was no architect, but became passionately interested in landscape gardening and set to work under the tuition of Eric Savill, Deputy Surveyor of Windsor Park. Over the years, he laid out a meticulous arrangement of gardens with great banks of rhododendrons and azaleas. Expertise came easily to him; he became an addict of flower shows, able to conduct a witty and erudite correspondence with Lady Stair, written entirely in the dog-latin of shrub terminology.

The 1930s opened with six quiet, uneventful years, the natural

The Duke of York, partnered by Sir Louis Greig, when he was defeated in the first round of the men's doubles at Wimbledon in 1926. The Duke was a fine lefthanded player who had already won the RAF double championships with Greig in 1920.

outcome of a growing family, in the comparatively wealthy seclusion of upper-class society. The Yorks, however, did not return to 'society'. While the Duke hunted with the Pytchley or the Whaddon, 'Chips' Channon noted later: 'He had few friends and was almost entirely dependent on [the Duchess of York], whom he worshipped. She was his will power, his all. He was an affectionate father and a loyal friend to the very few people he liked.' He was a fine shot, though not in the same exceptional class as his father, a good, even reckless, horseman and a sagacious fly-fisherman. Country sports, especially in Scotland, occupied a large part of his leisure, and he was not mealy-mouthed in defence of them. However much the Duke was trying to break down social barriers elsewhere, he lived in private the full life of an English aristocrat.

Political debates passed him by. Far too well schooled in the constitutional niceties to do more than express a private concern – like George v at the prospect of a flood-tide of Socialism in 1923 – he was content to sit occasionally in the gallery of the House of Commons, to watch for example the debates during the General Strike, or the slow assumption by the Labour Party of a Parliamentary road to the millenium. On the other hand, privately he expressed at least one total commitment. His faith was simple and fixed on a clear, low Anglican note. He did not mourn the loss of the revised Prayer Book in 1928 but his heart was lifted by witnessing the Presbyterian reunion. The bare white-washed church at Crathie, where the family worshipped while staying in Balmoral, suited his taste perfectly – extempore prayers, individual dedication, rather than high ceremony. His religion contained little philosophy but was based on order and discipline, and a sound sense of the importance of good works. Through his maturity, it reflected what he had written after confirmation: 'I have always remembered that day as one on which I took a great step in life. I took the Holy Communion on Easter Day alone with my father and mother, my elder brother and my sister. It was so very nice, having a small service, quite alone like that, only the family.'

Outside, the storms of the 1930s had begun and new experiments in government to control them: in Germany, the rise of Hitler, in France the Popular Front, in the United States the New Deal; later, in Spain, the tensions led to civil war. Less

68

affected by the clash of ideology between Fascism and Communism, Britain seemed wedded to a middle way, to balanced budgets, cautious social and foreign policy, widespread antagonism to European entanglements. But the League of Nations and the Locarno Pact succumbed in the 1930s to a series of disasters leaving the cloak of collective security in tatters. To replace it, some looked to imperial defence, or a form of Atlanticism; others to closer *entente* with France against Germany. These were not worries for the Duke of York, whose life seemed less and less publicly engaged. But, as the Duke and Duchess drove in the procession, during the Silver Jubilee in 1935 amidst the outpouring of loyalty to the monarchy which astonished the old and sick King, a prophetic cry was heard – 'There goes the hope of England.' George V was laid low again in December and, after a tremulous broadcast to the Empire on Christmas Day, he died at Sandringham in mid-January 1936.

The Duke and Duchess of York and their children driving in the Silver Jubilee procession of George V. A voice in the crowd cried out, 'There goes the hope of England'.

3 Abdication 1936

EDWARD VIII WAS PROCLAIMED KING on 20 January 1936. The Prince Charming of the decade, he was hailed by *The Times* as heir to Edward VII rather than George V: 'Men, not books are his library and he has the same power to learn from them.' Boyish-looking yet sophisticated, lively, febrile and original, he appeared to be a monarch appropriate to the modern age.

To his younger brother, he was the object of great affection but also envy and sometimes disapproval. From their nursery days, Edward had excelled where Albert struggled. In public and on social occasions, he possessed all the assurance and spontaneity the other lacked. He had seen the whole Empire in his tours during the 1920s and won a measure of independence from their father. 'All his life', the Duke of York told Mrs Baldwin in 1936, 'he had been outshone by his brilliant brother and there had been times when as a boy he had felt envious that eighteen months should make such a difference.' But they got on well together and, in spite of long absences of contact, shared the same sense of humour. 'There is a lovely story going round', York wrote during the King's illness in 1928, 'that the reason of your rushing home is that in the event of anything happening to papa, I am going to bag the throne in your absence! Just like the Middle Ages!'

George V, however, had watched the Prince of Wales grow to maturity with increasingly gloomy predictions. Gratified at his popularity, especially in the Dominions, he deplored the Prince's levity and flippancy, and his generally sceptical view of the rigid routine which the King regarded as an essential buttress to the mystique of monarchy. Irregularity of dress seemed to signify unorthodox attitudes. Their relations might have been easier if the Prince had married. The King, after all, mellowed towards the Duke of York and doted on his grandchildren – Princess Elizabeth was even allowed to stay during his convalesence at Bognor Regis. Instead, the old man pointed the contrast, even when congratulating York on his marriage: 'You have always been so sensible and easy to work with and you have always been ready to listen to my advice and to agree with my opinions about people and things, that I feel we have always got on very well together. Very different to dear David.'

After 1931, saddened by the death of trusted friends such as

PREVIOUS PAGES
Two unhappy men:
LEFT Edward VIII leaving Windsor Castle after his abdication speech;
RIGHT The new King, George VI. drives to his London home.

OPPOSITE The debonair Prince of Wales in the uniform of the Welsh Guards, 1932.

George v with Princess Elizabeth at Balmoral, 1928. He was far more at ease with his grandchildren than he had ever been with his sons.

his private secretary, Lord Stamfordham, and irritated by a succession of illnesses, George v retreated from the rapidly changing world he found hard to understand into a regime of habits governed by rigid attention to detail. Punctuality, meticulous dress and the forms of religious observance ranked high in his priorities. Queen Mary shielded him from many things likely to upset him but she could not prevent his clashing with the Prince of Wales, nor was the latter able to confide in either parent. He reacted angrily against what he felt to be his father's autocratic behaviour and insistence on red tape. In particular, he complained of exclusion from knowledge of state affairs and of the extravagant style in which the royal houses were maintained.

The first was a genuine grievance, echoing the mistakes made in the education of Edward vii, and since inexperience of politics played a large part in the ending of Edward viii's

74

reign, George V must bear some of the blame. The outcry against Sandringham – 'that bloody dull 'ouse' as J.H. Thomas called it – was a product of the need for economy after 1931 and a protest against the old-fashioned management of the royal estates; but it also reflected the antagonism between his own Household at Fort Belvedere and the officials of his father's Court. When he became King, he asked the Duke of York to lead an enquiry into how best to introduce economies and although some of the cuts cost York much pain, they discussed the matter together and still saw eye to eye. The introduction of new servants and officials went less harmoniously.

To the public, Edward VIII seemed to be heir to what was best in the British monarchy, possessing as he did the virtues of uprightness, commonsense, sympathy and lack of condescension which his father had exemplified, with none of the stuffiness. It was not clear, outside the circle of his friends, how far he wanted actually to change the monarchy and lift it out of what he believed to be the paralysis of upper-class associations. He desired to be a popular and populist King but he scarcely appreciated the difficulties, partly from lack of experience of the working of British institutions and partly because he over-rated the power of the monarchy itself. His aims needed time and political strength and he was to have neither.

Various forms of opposition to Edward VIII existed, even before he came to the throne. He started with a certain lack of confidence among the ministers of the National Government, which the late King had done nothing to dispel, by such warnings as 'After I am dead, the boy will ruin himself within twelve months.' What had been said to the Archbishop, Cosmo Gordon Lang, and Baldwin, related chiefly to Mrs Simpson, but until the question of marriage was raised, her appearance could scarcely cause the Prime Minister to intervene. (In fact, Baldwin's acquaintance dated from 1927 when he accompanied the Prince of Wales to Canada. They had been on terms of some trust, although Baldwin's avuncular manner irritated the young man.) It was more a comment on Edward VIII's lack of application to his duties than his penchant for women which caused Baldwin to tell Clement Attlee, at the Accession Council, that he doubted if the new King 'would stay the course'. Other Ministers looked at him with less friendly eyes, but the majority

The Prince of Wales (in
tartan) with the Duke of
Kent and Mr and Mrs
Baldwin during his
Canadian tour. The Prince,
although friendly with
Baldwin, was irritated by
his avuncular attitude.

would probably have agreed with the Court official who wrote:
'There was no doubt of the young man's capacity for goodness.'

The troubles they feared were, at first, very general. His
actions clearly showed that he meant to *be* King; to reverse, if
necessary, over half a century of precedents in which the
monarchy had dutifully echoed its ministers' words and
sentiments. There might be conflict if he disagreed with them
over a political issue, or a matter of foreign policy, such as the
response to German militarisation of the Rhineland in March
1936. But even if the King restricted himself to setting a different
sort of example, he might cause dissension because he was not
simply King of England. The nonconformist conscience, as
Lord Kemsley remarked during the Abdication crisis, was not
dead, at least in Wales, and a strong Protestant tradition survived in Scotland and Northern Ireland. Any whittling away
at the moral standards the monarchy was supposed to represent
would be matter for hostile comment. Edward VIII was also
King to Australian Catholics, French Canadians, Calvinist
Boer farmers, communities decades behind the permissive
climate of London. By 1936 the actual personality of the King
was not something easily separable from the symbolic attri-
butes of office. As the real links of Empire weakened, these
were emphasised, so that his actions had to be tailored to meet
the demands. Defects of character, or behaviour other than the

The Prince of Wales speaking to an unemployed man on his tour of the mining districts in 1929.

expected, thus became more damaging than in Edward VII's time. Moreover, as the prestige of monarchy became a counter-weight to Britain's declining power, it became essential, to governments who strove to retain control over the country's future, that the King should fulfil his appointed role.

A more specific ground of mistrust lay in the King's feelings about foreign affairs. He believed – as many politicians still did in 1936 – in co-existence with Germany and in the possibility of an agreement with Hitler. Hence his attempt, much resented by the Foreign Office, to persuade Eden to tone down British protests at the breach of the Locarno Pact and the Versailles Treaty, when German troops marched into the Rhineland. His friendliness towards the German Ambassadors in London, von Hoesch and Ribbentrop, caused uneasiness because of what the German government deduced about his attitude. There was no overt support of National Socialism here, but he did later visit Hitler, in November 1937 – a gesture highly unpopular in Britain and the United States – and German diplomatic docu-ments show that their Foreign Ministry set some store by his sympathy.

It could be argued that the King simply refused to admit that war was inevitable and, in seeking a bridge of understanding, stood no nearer Germany than Lord Halifax, Neville Chamber-lain or Geoffrey Dawson, editor of *The Times*. But the Cabinet

77

suspected by 1936 that Hitler was changing ground from his earlier view of Britain as a 'natural ally' to one in which she appeared, like France, as a 'hate-inspired antagonist, to whom the idea of a German colossus in the centre of Europe was a thorn in the flesh'. In 1934, the vitally important Defence Requirements Committee of the Cabinet had predicted that Germany was the long-term enemy. Subsequent re-armament policy had been decided with this warning in mind. The risk that, if war broke out, the King could be depicted by Germany as a possible sympathiser, was fully understood, and it was this, rather than his light-hearted attitude to security, which led to vetting of Foreign Office papers before they were sent down to Fort Belvedere.

The third worry was that the King was not married. The virtues required by convention included a wife and children. Yet when he met Mrs Simpson, and took her with him on a holiday in Austria, George V was so horrified that he consulted both Baldwin and Archbishop Lang. Mrs Simpson was vivacious, witty and exactly attuned to Edward VIII; it mattered little that she was American, but the overwhelming disadvant-age was that she was already married, with a divorced husband living. She figured prominently in Edward's entourage in 1935–6. They dined together, and she was well enough known to the Household for one official to write: 'Before her, the affairs of state sank into insignificance'; but it was not until the King chartered the yacht *Nahlin* for a Mediterranean cruise in the summer of 1936 that the world became interested. The two were photographed together, sometimes on lonely beaches, and reporters followed them all the way to Vienna and home. Tactfully the British Press restrained itself.

The King invited Mrs Simpson to Balmoral in the autumn, much to Queen Mary's displeasure, and met her at the station, leaving his brother to stand in for him at the opening of a new hospital wing in Aberdeen. A few sour comments appeared in Scottish newspapers. Much more resented, however, was the way he swept out Balmoral, this time with the advice of Mrs Simpson rather than the Duke of York, who began to feel that 'he had lost a friend and was rapidly losing a brother'. The Duke was unwilling to face the logic of these developments and looked to time and Queen Mary to soften them.

ABOVE The Prince of Wales and Mrs Simpson at Ascot in June, 1935.

The royal family was united in disapproval. Edward VIII, however, had not yet expressed his wish to marry Mrs Simpson, whose divorce was pronounced at Ipswich in October. The American and French newspapers gave the news banner head-lines but the British Press, bound by a gentlemen's agreement, kept silent. Deeply concerned at the dilemma posed by the forthcoming Coronation, a Christian ceremony in which the King's wife must become Queen, celebrated by a Church whose absolute rule was that Christian marriage lasted for life, Baldwin saw the King on 20 October; but the implications of the warning he delivered were not wholly clear nor did the King mention marriage. A series of meetings followed, in-volving Cabinet Ministers, the King's private secretary, Sir

Alexander Hardinge, and others of the inner political circle. As the Prime Minister tested opinion with such sources as the Governor General of Canada and leaders of the Labour Party, the numbers of people in the know steadily increased.

On 28 October, with a far-sighted interpretation of his duty, Hardinge spoke to the Duke of York and suggested that even abdication was not impossible. The Duke listened 'with consternation and incredulity'. Meanwhile, the heads of the Civil Service and the Chancellor of the Exchequer concocted an official submission to be made by the Prime Minister which looked remarkably like an ultimatum: the King must cease his association with Mrs Simpson or the Government would resign. Wisely, Baldwin refused. It was not his intention to drive the King out but to make him see his duties clearly. Serious political risks were opening up: Labour Party and Trade Union opinion opposed such a marriage (if their leaders were correct in their analysis.) The Press could not be held in check for much longer; and there was a distinct chance that the King's Proctor, an official of the divorce court, might intervene before Mrs Simpson's decree *nisi* became absolute, on the grounds of collusion.

Hardinge sent an outspoken letter of warning to the King who reacted angrily, apparently unaware both of how far things had gone and of how the political world had hardened against his wishes. Indications from Dominion Prime Ministers supported Hardinge. The Australian High Commissioner, Stanley Bruce, told Baldwin: 'If there was any question of marriage, the King would have to go, as far as Australia was concerned.' Lord Tweedsmuir reported: 'Canada is the most puritanical part of the Empire and cherishes very much the Victorian standards of private life ...' The heads of the British Legion hinted that the King's popularity could not survive, even among ex-servicemen.

The Duke of York watched with growing alarm, but he could not discuss the situation with his brother – 'He is very difficult to see, and when one does, he wants to talk about other matters.' Queen Mary needed help as much as he did. Even so, until mid-November, no one seriously believed that the King would fail to find a way out. Then, during his second and far graver interview with Baldwin, he said that he meant to go through

with it: 'I have looked at it from all sides, and I mean to abdicate and marry Mrs Simpson.'

Various attempts were made to change his mind. Queen Mary argued with him but made no impression; he would not give up the woman he loved. Nor was he shaken by the pleading of his brothers; and he was too honest to play for time, and wait until after the Coronation to marry. Walter Monckton, his legal adviser, thought him resolved to go, and the Law Officers began to draw up a timetable for voluntary abdication.

Not all of those who gave advice shared the same interests in preserving political stability. In the *Daily Mail*, Lord Rothermere was making capital out of the contrast between the King's openly expressed sympathy for the plight of Welsh miners and the government's inability to cure unemployment. There was a danger that a King's party might grow among

The King with his two nieces and the Duke of York. Edward's friendship with his brother suffered at the Abdication, and he was discouraged from ever returning to live in Britain.

OVERLEAF LEFT The development of aircraft between 1910-35, from paintings by G.H.Davis. RIGHT Milestones of the First World War.

1910

ROE TRIPLANE

DUNNE

1911

BRISTOL BIPLANE

MARTIN-HANDYSIDE

1912

THE FIRST AMPHIBIAN

THE FIRST CABIN AEROPLANE

1913

EARLY FIGHTING AIRCRAFT

"B.E.2C"

AVRO "504"

1914

THE SOPWITH SEAPLANE WHICH FIRST WON THE SCHNEIDER TROPHY FOR GREAT BRITAIN

SOPWITH

SOPWITH "CAMEL"

"F.E.2B"

"R.E.8"

D.H.4

BRISTOL "FIGHTER"

"S.E.5A"

HANDLEY-PAGE "0400"

SHORT SEAPLANE

"F2A" FLYING BOAT

OUTSTANDING AIRCRAFT OF THE GREAT WAR

dissident Conservatives which became vividly clear with a proposal from Esmond Harmsworth for a morganatic marriage: that is, one in which Mrs Simpson would not become Queen. Churchill, caught up by emotional feelings for the threatened King, lent his authority to the campaign, and Lord Beaverbrook, proprietor of the *Daily Express*, busied himself making trouble for the government.

When the King put the morganatic proposal to Baldwin he was told that the government must consider it formally and, since it required legislation, so must the Dominions. Unaware perhaps of their views and the fact that he must constitutionally be bound by such formal advice, the King consented. For a short while he hoped for a solution. Meanwhile, Attlee and Sinclair, leaders of the Labour and Liberal Parties, pledged themselves not to form a government if Baldwin resigned over this issue; Churchill, on the other hand, replied equivocally.

The Dominion Prime Ministers' replies left no leeway. From South Africa, General Hertzog stated that abdication would be a lesser shock than morganatic marriage. De Valera believed that Edward VIII could no longer remain King of Eire. Canadians feared a dangerous division of opinion. Lyons, the Australian Premier, spoke most strongly: 'It would run counter to the best popular conception of the Royal Family.' The King was shaken but not convinced. He was more disturbed by the Press, which broke silence on 3 December, following a sermon by the Bishop of Bradford, in which he had expressed the wish (nothing to do with Mrs Simpson) that the King would show 'more positive signs of his awareness' of the need for God's grace at the Coronation.

The Cabinet met and vetoed morganatic marriage. Mrs Simpson left for the South of France, urged on by the King who feared a possible demonstration against her. Some attempts were made there to induce her to withdraw altogether but the King was firmly set and refused to countenance them. During the first week of December the balance hung between a constitutional crisis and abdication. The King produced another scheme: he wished to broadcast to the nation and ask for time for the public to reflect. This horrified the Cabinet and his own supporters, for its constitutional impropriety, and very correctly he did not mention it again. During the last manœuvrings,

84

however, the formation of a King's party of perhaps forty MPs and peers, with Churchill as a potential leader, appeared imminent. Shrewdly, Beaverbrook, who understood that the King would not chance such a crisis, warned Churchill, 'Our cock won't fight.' The King finally decided to abdicate; during the weekend of 5–6 December, a great deal of hostile opinion made itself felt in the constituencies, and the King's party simply faded away.

The Duke of York, all this time, was being prepared in the greatest secrecy for his unwilling inheritance, advised by Baldwin and consoled by Queen Mary, who never wavered in her stern belief that the King was deserting his duty. The Dukes of York and Gloucester shared her feelings; they disliked Mrs Simpson and, happily married themselves, failed to comprehend the King's passion. When they dined together at the Fort on 8 December, for the first time in three years, they were nevertheless amazed at the light-hearted skill with which the King carried off the dismal evening. 'The King appeared happy and gay, as if he were looking forward to his honeymoon', Baldwin told the Cabinet afterwards. The Duke of York remarked, unbelievingly, to Monckton, 'and this is the man we are going to lose'.

The end came for Edward VIII with the signature of the Instrument of Abdication and the journey across the Channel on the destroyer *Fury*. For the Duke of York it was a harsh, unwelcome beginning. Admittedly, Edward had done his best to smooth the transition, by asking Baldwin, in the debate in the House of Commons, to affirm that relations between them had always been good. In a masterly speech, Baldwin gave the ex-King the most favourable interpretation at each stage of the tangled chain of events and lifted the crisis from the level of rumour and scandal onto the high dramatic plane on which it has since been viewed. Other agencies were at work, also, to protect the Crown and the succession. Geoffrey Dawson, eager to be at the centre of affairs, ordered *The Times* to shift its emphasis before the news became public: 'Try to spread the loyalty of our readers a little more widely over the Royal Family.' More important, Baldwin who had been close to resigning in the autumn, now stayed, to the ill-concealed impatience of Chamberlain, 'to see the new King into the saddle'.

NO. 17,134   FIFTY-SIXTH YEAR   LONDON : THURSDAY, DECEMBER 10, 1936   ONE PENNY

The Evening News

LARGEST EVENING NET SALE IN THE WORLD

BROADCASTING PAGE 6

LATE EXTRA

THE KING ABDICATES

"My Final and Irrevocable Decision": The Duke of York Succeeds To The Throne at Once

"I CAN NO LONGER DISCHARGE MY HEAVY TASK WITH EFFICIENCY"

Abdication Instrument Signed To-day With The Three Royal Brothers as Witnesses

MESSAGE READ TO PARLIAMENT

"My Mind Is Made Up: Further Delay Cannot But Be Most Injurious"

King Edward the Eighth has abdicated his Throne. He announced his decision in the following message which he sent to Parliament this afternoon and which was read by the Speaker to the House of Commons:

After long and anxious consideration I have determined to renounce the Throne to which I succeeded on the death of my Father, and I am now communicating this My final and irrevocable decision.

Realising as I do the gravity of this step, I can only hope that I shall have the understanding of My peoples in the decision I have taken and the reasons which have led me to take it.

I will not enter now into My private feelings, but I would beg that it should be remembered that the burden which constantly rests upon the shoulders of a sovereign is so heavy that it can only be borne in circumstances different from those in which I now find Myself.

I conceive that I am not overlooking the duty that rests on Me to place in the forefront the public interest, when I declare that I am conscious that I can no longer discharge this heavy task with efficiency or with satisfaction to Myself.

THE ABDICATION INSTRUMENT

I have accordingly this morning executed an Instrument of Abdication in the terms following:

"I, Edward the VIII of Gt. Britain, Ireland and the Dominions beyond the Seas, King, Emperor of India, do hereby declare my irrevocable determination to renounce the Throne for Myself and for my descendants, and My desire that effect should be given to this Instrument of Abdication immediately

"In token whereof I have hereunto set My hand this tenth day of December, nineteen hundred and thirty-six, in the presence of the witnesses whose signatures are subscribed.

(Signed)   **Edward R. I."**

My execution of this Instrument has been witnessed by My three brothers, Their Royal Highnesses The Duke of York, the Duke of Gloucester and the Duke of Kent.

I deeply appreciate the spirit which has actuated the appeals which have been made to Me to take a different decision, and I have before reaching my final determination most fully pondered over them.

But my mind is made up. Moreover, further delay cannot but be most injurious to the peoples whom I have tried to serve as Prince of Wales and as King and whose future happiness and prosperity are the constant wish of My heart.

I take My leave of them in the confident hope that the course which I have thought it right to follow is that which is best for the stability of the Throne and Empire, and the happiness of My peoples.

NO DELAY OF ANY KIND"

I am deeply sensible of the consideration which they have always extended to Me, both before and after my accession to the Throne, and which I know they will extend in full measure to My successor.

I am most anxious that there should be no delay of any kind in giving effect to the Instrument which I have executed and that all necessary steps should be taken immediately to secure that my lawful successor, My brother, His Royal Highness the Duke of York, should ascend the Throne.

EDWARD R.I.

The King To Go Abroad

The Press Association learns that King Edward will leave the country immediately after signing his Act of Abdication — probably to-morrow night.

King Edward will renounce with the Throne all his titles. It is probable that the Duke of York will confer a high peerage, probably a dukedom, on him.

King Edward's destination is being kept a close secret. But it is stated on what is described as good authority, that it is not a British Dominion or a British possession.

It is believed that there will be no alteration in the Coronation date fixed for May 12.

Proclamation on Saturday

It is authoritatively stated that the Accession Council will be held on Saturday morning. The new King will be proclaimed on Saturday afternoon.

A change in monarchy is the one occasion upon which all the members of the Privy Council with the Lord Mayor, Aldermen and other representatives of the City are summoned to be present.

New King May Be George VI

It is understood that the Duke of York has not yet made a decision as to what title he will take. It is considered likely that he will choose to be known as George the Sixth rather than Albert the First.

Sensational Speech By Mr. Baldwin

"THE KING SAID : 'I AM GOING TO MARRY MRS. SIMPSON . . . I AM PREPARED TO GO'"

MR. BALDWIN made a sensational speech in the House of Commons after King Edward's message had been read.

Here are points from the speech which is reported fully on **Page Three:**

No more grave message has ever been received by Parliament.

His Majesty, as Prince of Wales, has honoured me with his friendship for many years, which I value.

When we said good-bye on Tuesday night at Fort Belvedere we both knew and felt and said to each other that that friendship, far from being impaired by the discussions of this last week, bound us more closely together than it ever had and would last for life.

"We Must Settle It"

I felt bound to speak to the King in view of the volume of correspondence which was coming to me in October.

I told the King that I wanted to talk it over with him as a friend to see if I could be of help to him.

He said: "You and I must settle this matter together. I will not have anyone else interfering."

I saw him the next time on November 16. I spoke to him on that occasion for twenty minutes on the question of marriage.

I told him that I did not think that a particular marriage was one that would receive the approbation of the country.

I pointed out to him that the position of the King's wife was different from the position of the wife of any other citizen in the country.

"I Am Prepared To Go"

Then His Majesty said to me, and I have his permission to repeat it. He said that he wanted to tell me something that he had long wanted to tell me.

He said : "I am going to marry Mrs. Simpson, and I am prepared to go."

I said : "Sir, that is most grievous news. It is impossible for me to make any comment on that to-day."

He sent for me again on November 21. In the meantime a suggestion had been made to me that a possible compromise might be arranged.

The compromise was that the King

---

should marry and that Parliament should pass an Act enabling the lady to be the King's wife without the position of Queen.

When I saw His Majesty on November 25 he asked me if the proposition had been put before me and I said Yes.

I told him that I had not had a considered opinion, but if he asked me my personal reaction informally, my reaction was that Parliament would never be the Bill.

Before The Cabinet

I asked him if he desired me to put forward the matter formally. He said he desired. I told him it will mean my putting it before the whole Cabinet and communicating with the Prime Ministers of the Dominions.

He said that was his wish, and I told him that I would do it.

It is difficult to realise that His Majesty is not a boy. Although he looks so young he is a matured man with great experience of life and of the world.

He wanted Jo go in circumstances which would make the succession of his brother as little difficult as possible.

He stayed down at Fort Belvedere because he said he was not going to come to London while these things were in dispute because of the cheering crowds.

A Pencil Note

Mr. Baldwin then produced what he said was a pencil note sent to him by the King this morning.

The note said that the Duke of York and the King "have always been on the best of terms as brothers and the King is confident the Duke deserves and will receive the support of the whole Empire."

Continuing, Mr. Baldwin said: This crisis has arisen now rather than later from that frankness of His Majesty's character which is one of his many attractions.

This evening I shall ask leave to bring in the necessary Bill which will be available to members as soon as the House has ordered the Bill to be printed.

Mr. Baldwin said that last night, in reply to a minute which was sent to the King, the Cabinet received a message from him regretting that he was unable to alter his decision.

This Night Of History

Parliament heard to-night the most momentous pronouncement it has ever heard.

The House of Commons, filled as it has rarely been filled, heard afterwards Mr. Baldwin's sensational speech, reported in full on **Page Three**

Speeches in the House of Lords, including one by the Archbishop of York, are given on

At Fort Belvedere this night the Duke of York is dining with the King.

Mrs. Simpson Told By Phone

Mrs. Simpson was told the news over the telephone at Cannes to-night. It had earlier been announced on her behalf that the King was definitely not visiting Cannes or the Riviera. See Page NINE.

Crowds scenes are described on *Page Four.*

The Duke of York,

The Duchess of York.

Their elder daughter, Princess Elizabeth.

Early in January 1937, the Baldwins spent a weekend at Sandringham – 'a family gathering, with the Bishop of Jarrow as preacher, the only other visitor' – and gave much sound advice. So too did Hardinge, who became the new King's private secretary.

But the full weight fell on him. From a mood of total aversion to the idea at the start, he had come to accept his fate. 'If the worst happens', he wrote to Sir Godfrey Thomas, assistant private secretary, in late November, 'and I have to take over, you can be assured that I will do my best to clear up the inevitable mess, if the whole fabric does not crumble under the shock and strain of it all.' He was away in Scotland, at one remove from events, when the papers broke the story, and even in London found himself prone to a sense of unreality. The truth came home after seeing the lawyers: he explained the schedule of abdication to his mother and then, in his own words, 'broke down and sobbed like a child'. For a nervous, withdrawn man, the strain was terrible. Silently, he watched 'a perfectly calm D[avid]' sign the Instrument of Abdication. 'It was a dreadful moment and one never to be forgotten by those present. ... I later went to London where I found a large crowd outside my house, cheering madly. I was overwhelmed.'

Finally, 'When D and I said goodbye, we kissed, parted as freemasons, and he bowed to me as King.' George VI, as he styled himself now, faced the Accession Council, and the Privy Councillors, many of whom were to be his ministers during the next sixteen years. His first act was to grant his brother the title of a royal duke, HRH the Duke of Windsor. On the Sunday after the Proclamation, prayers were said across the Commonwealth for a new royal family.

OPPOSITE The Abdication story in the *Evening News*, December 10, 1936.

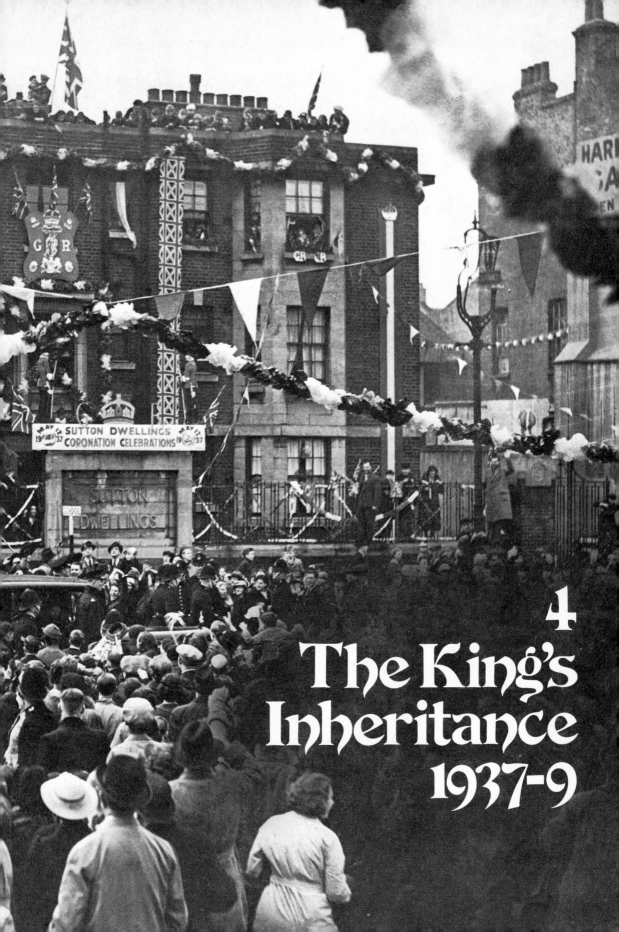

4

The King's
Inheritance
1937-9

O N THE FIRST NIGHT of his reign, during a long conversation with his cousin Lord Mountbatten, George VI said 'Dickie, this is absolutely terrible. I never wanted this to happen; I'm quite unprepared for it. David has been trained for this all his life. I've never even seen a state paper; I'm only a naval officer, it's the only thing I know about.' Mountbatten replied that, according to his own father, George V had said exactly the same when the Duke of Clarence died. But George V had risen to the rank of Captain after fifteen years' full-time service in the navy. His son was inexperienced in the ways of leadership and political life and, ignoring his own youthful predicament, George V had made no provision for him to be enlightened. George VI had a short time, over Christmas at Sandringham, to adjust; but that could be only temporary, despite his heartfelt plea to Baldwin: 'I am new to the job but I hope that time will be allowed to me to make amends for what has happened.'

He possessed, of course, a basic understanding of his new formal duties and of the scope and privileges of the monarchy. His Cambridge tutors had done their work even in one short academic year. From Dicey's *Law of the Constitution* and Bagehot's *English Constitution*, and from his father's meticulous correctness towards his ministers, George VI had learned principles already useful to him during the Abdication crisis. Bagehot had emphasised the nineteenth-century idea that the King should express the values of family life and sound social morality. The behaviour of Edward VII had been regarded as an aberration precisely because, in Bagehot's words, 'We have come to believe that it is natural to have a virtuous sovereign, and that domestic virtues are as likely to be found on thrones, as they are eminent when there.' In such matters, George VI was already armoured, but other precepts were harder: 'Royalty is a government in which the attention of the nation is con-centrated on one person doing interesting things.' How could that, reminiscent of Edward VIII's populist aims, be reconciled with the more congenial words which followed: 'Its mystery is its life; we must not bring in the daylight upon magic'?

All this, however, was only theory. In practice, there was the right to be consulted, the right to encourage, the right to warn. Through twenty-six often uneasy years, George V had given strong and usually sound advice to four Prime Ministers who

had followed it when it coincided with government policy and respected it when it did not. He had, in the last resort, made his own choice between Baldwin and Lord Curzon, as successor to Bonar Law in 1923; in the crisis of 1931 he had noticeably affected not only Ramsay MacDonald's decision to head a National Government after the Labour Cabinet resigned, but also Baldwin's earlier resolve not to commit the Conservatives to a coalition. Whatever George VI's personal qualities, and however much sympathetic observers like Thomas Jones might say 'All who know the new King say he will grow into the likeness of his father', such maturity of judgment could come only with time.

Thus the immediate problem of the damage done to the institution of monarchy by the Abdication was not the greatest which George VI had to face. Indeed that proved to have been grossly exaggerated. A few demonstrations took place at the time; the British Union of Fascists had offered particularly un-welcome support to Edward VIII and there had been groups in front of Buckingham Palace, chanting 'Down with Baldwin, we want the King.' Talk of 'the King's party' muddied the waters of party politics a little and in the Commons, James Maxton, leading the remnant of the Independent Labour Party, moved an amendment to the Abdication Bill: 'We are doing a wrong and foolish thing if, as a House, we do not seize the opportunity ... of establishing in our land a completely democratic form of government which does away with old monarchical institutions and the hereditary principle.' The republican amendment, however, was lost by 403 votes to five, and a powerful reaction followed in 1937. George VI's courage, simplicity and obvious dedication to public service, offered no grounds for criticism. Many of the ex-King's friends deserted him, inspiring a savage poem by Osbert Sitwell, entitled *Rat Week*, and Churchill, in a serious setback to his career, was virtually ostracised. In many ways, the spotlight on the mon-archy seemed to have awakened interest rather than caused a revulsion against it. George VI's earliest actions, like his choice of title, were designed to show that Edward VIII's reign had been an aberration. Many of the old patterns of Court life were revived. But the temporary assumption of his father's style of kingship could only mask a much larger problem.

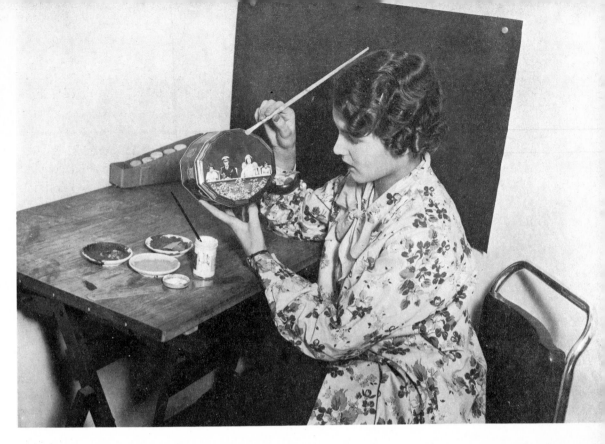

By common consent of the political parties and the constitutional historians, scope no longer existed for the monarch to busy himself with the minutiae of public and foreign affairs. Whereas Edward VII's ministers had seen him as part of their calculations either, like Haldane and Fisher, to bid for his support or, like Balfour, to ignore it, those of George V had made their decisions without considering his standpoint. It could hardly be said that they were more than glad if he concurred, regretful if he appeared upset. Certain fields of policy such as the making of treaties and questions of sovereignty still fell within the royal purview, as did the prerogative of mercy and the death penalty. But in practice these too were ministerial responsibilities. An absolute convention of compliance had been gradually established since the days of Queen Victoria, which Edward VIII also accepted; he did not attempt to insist, for example, on broadcasting before the Abdication.

But this did not mean that kingship was purely ornamental. The King needed no longer to be a leader of 'society' like Edward VII, but he was a social figure of substantial importance. Millions of people who had never met him made vague but

Within a few hours of the news of the Abdication new designs were ready for the coronation tins.

ABOVE The royal luncheon
at the Guildhall to celebrate
the Coronation, by
Frank Salisbury.

RIGHT The Coronation
portrait of
King George VI
by Frank Salisbury.

implicit claims on his authority and, insofar as they knew what 'allegiance' meant, took it to be a reflection of their own ideals. On the political level, the King was more than a name. As Duke of York, George VI had been useful to the Foreign Office in the Balkans in 1923, just as the Prince of Wales had served the interests of the Dominions and Colonial Offices in the 1920s. But the meaning attached to monarchy by different classes or countries within the Commonwealth changed continually. During George VI's own lifetime, the old dichotomy of Liberals and Conservatives had been broken by the Labour Party. As Edward VIII had seen, there could be no permanent stability in the social position, nor even in the moral role, exemplified by George V. It was true that he had failed to find an alternative to meet the demands for a presidential, democratic figurehead, a representative not tied by wealth and upbringing to a particular social class; yet some of the methods he adopted, the greater informality and openness, the absence of cant and the drive against conspicuous spending, had proved highly popular. Afterwards, the 'magic and mystery' of kingship looked sadly out of date. Against this, George VI's search to resemble his father, as well as his style of life and leisure, raised the question whether he could be flexible enough, or creative enough, to embody a modern approach to monarchy. Could he meet the challenge implicit in the deep divisions of wealth and class only too evident in the 1930s?

Lacking knowledge of the majority of politicians, public men and Church leaders, and especially those of the Commonwealth, he had to rely at first on his Prime Minister and his Household officials. The Prime Minister no longer wrote a daily report of the proceedings in Parliament in his own hand (a grave loss to political historians) but he corresponded frequently with the King and saw him regularly. Baldwin, three times Prime Minister, and survivor of a dozen crises, was invaluable in the months before his retirement in May 1937. Wise and unpompous, he seemed peculiarly in touch with public opinion; he was trusted by the Labour Party to whom, in Opposition, he had always shown respect. He advised the King to extend his acquaintance and offered to give a series of small dinner parties for him to meet members of the House of Commons. At one, for example, in December 1938, there were present A. V.

Alexander, Chuter Ede, Arthur Greenwood, David Grenfell and Tom Williams, a roll-call of Labour leaders. Long after his retirement, Baldwin continued to advise the King: he hurried back from holiday in France on 22 September 1938 just before Chamberlain reached Godesberg and the second disastrous interview with Hitler. As late as Christmas 1939, the King still corresponded with him – in that case to acknowledge help with his annual broadcast, a famous speech with its prophetic image 'I spoke to the man who stood at the gate of the year.'

Neville Chamberlain was a more dominant and masterful Prime Minister, his prestige rooted firmly in administrative office and the chancellorship of the Exchequer since 1931. His policy in foreign affairs brooked no delay, even from Eden, the Foreign Secretary, and where Cabinet Ministers could do little but consent, there was no room for advice from a new King. Yet Chamberlain was careful for the proprieties and genuinely sought to keep the King informed; and for that lonely, often misunderstood leader, the King was one of the few in whom he could confide. Their exchanges of letters after Munich and on Chamberlain's resignation in 1940 show that George VI sympathised with what he had tried to do.

The King could be certain of the support of his family. Queen Mary showed her pride in the son who had lived up to his duty, and the new Queen Elizabeth sustained him in this sphere as she had done so sympathetically before. Archbishop Lang proved to be a less welcome support: fervently determined to pursue the moral issue to its limit, he had made a peculiarly vindictive broadcast about the Duke of Windsor, which earned him the doggerel riposte:

> My Lord Archbishop, what a scold you are
> And when a man's down, how bold you are
> Of Christian charity how scant you are
> You old Lang swine, how full of Cantuar.

His paternal attitude towards the King was seen as unhealthily archaic and he became an embarrassment when he tried, in the same broadcast, to explain about the King's stammer.

Among the Court officials, there lacked anyone of the calibre of Stamfordham who had taught George V, in his own words, 'how to be a King'. Hardinge, firm and upright, remained as

OVERLEAF Queen Elizabeth photographed by Cecil Beaton in 1939, on the terrace of Buckingham Palace.

private secretary until 1943 and Lord Wigram, who had served George V, was recalled as permanent Lord in Waiting. But these appointments had a divisive aspect because they were the antithesis of Edward VIII's Household: in the words of one diarist, they represented 'the most powerful and rigorous ceremonial machine', who hedged the new King round. The dismissal of Lord Brownlow, whose only offence was to have served Edward VIII well, was a bad omen; it happened without George VI's knowledge.

Fears that the new King might become a cipher were echoed in the first half of 1937 in the Press, which also circulated rumours that he was physically inadequate for the demands of the Coronation and that he might become a recluse. 'Chips' Channon – a prejudiced source of information – recorded his anger at the refusal of the title Royal Highness to the Duchess of Windsor on her marriage to the Duke in June and added: 'The present King and Queen are popular, very, and increasingly so, but they have no message for the Labour Party who believe them, and rightly, I fear, to be but the puppets of a palace clique. Certainly they are too hemmed in by the territorial aristocracy, and have all the faults and virtues which Edward VIII lacked in this particular field.'

There was, understandably, animus against the Duke and Duchess of Windsor. Some members of the Cabinet were reluctant to see him awarded a pension unless he undertook not to return to Britain, and one reason advanced for giving him the title of royal duke was that he could sit in neither House of Parliament. The fact that he wrote articles for newspapers to supplement his income, gave offence to conservatives, and the visit to Germany, in November 1937, just before going to the United States, was resented by liberal thinkers on both sides of the Atlantic. George VI's nature, however, was not vindictive. In the question of a title for the Duchess he only followed his government's advice. His own feelings showed more clearly in September 1939 when the Duke asked to be of service in the war. Touchy matters of precedence, and fears for the Duchess's reception in England, precluded a job at home but with tact and firmness the King persuaded his brother to join the staff of the military mission to France.

In less than two years of peace, the King could hardly do more

than establish himself. He gave an impression of steadily growing confidence in public, despite the vestigial embarrassment of the stammer. Channon noted at the state opening of Parliament: 'The King seemed quite at ease.' In front lay the Coronation, arranged long before, for May 1937, which was to go ahead as scheduled, though for a different King. Normally, eighteen months elapse after an accession, and in order to accomplish the Coronation in time, George VI was faced with six months of accelerated work and the advice of his Household that, because of the overload, the Durbar in Delhi, planned for the winter of 1937–8, should be postponed. This course had the additional advantage that it would keep the King in Britain until the echoes of 1936 had died away. Against them, the Secretary of State for India and the Viceroy argued that the King's presence in India was necessary to maintain loyalty to the imperial throne and to offset some of the hostility of the Congress Party, who were demanding independence or at least some of the regional autonomy of the 1935 Government of India Act. The King wished to go but he admitted the cogency of the arguments against and he gave way. Later, the international situation made it difficult to arrange the Durbar and he never did see India. But he knew enough about the political storms of the sub-continent to discount much of what was said about the power of one King to affect the destiny of its three million inhabitants.

Archbishop Lang intended, as part of his 'return to religion' crusade, to make the most of the Coronation as a supreme religious festival. The King, head of the Church and the Empire, fully concurred. The emotions raised during 1936 were to be channelled and redirected; the public was to be incorporated, if not physically, at least by radio and film, and the Westminster authorities were persuaded to wire the Abbey for the first sound, though not television, broadcast. Certain changes had to be made in the ancient order of ceremony, as a result of Dominion sensibilities. The oath had been a matter of endless dispute in the Irish negotiations of 1921 and the King was no longer, since the statute of Westminster, King of a single realm but of Great Britain, Canada, Australia and so on. Moreover, how was he to promise to maintain the Protestant faith when large numbers of his Dominion and British subjects were

Catholic? Malcolm MacDonald, the Dominions Secretary, was responsible for the finding of acceptable formulae, such as 'the true profession of the Gospel'.

In the Abbey, on that splendid day, among representatives of the nation and of the whole Commonwealth, one guest described 'the shaft of sunlight, catching the King's golden tunic as he sat for the crowning; the kneeling Bishops drawn up like a flight of geese; and then, the loveliest moment of all, the swirl when the peeresses put on their coronets – a thousand white gloved arms, sparkling with jewels'. The dedication and true faith of the King and Queen were obvious to all, for they made of the ceremony a clear consecration before God. The King's voice mercifully held steady throughout. Then followed the procession, the naval review, Empire Day; the whole capital *en fête*. The Press gave full scope to the events, and especially to the young Princesses, who shared in a new phenomenon – the growing adulation of the royal family as a whole.

George VI's performance of his public duties was adequate and often inspiring. But the Abdication and the Coronation had helped to obscure for months the threat developing in Europe. The aggressive intentions and armoured might of Germany had grown at enormous speed since the withdrawal from the League of Nations at the end of 1933. Until that date, Japanese ambitions in the Pacific and mainland China appeared to be more pressing dangers. It was the defence of British prestige and commercial interests in Shanghai, Hong Kong and Malaya which stimulated the Chiefs of Staff to demand the abrogation of the Ten Year Rule (under which defence planning was conducted on the basis that no major war was to be expected for ten years), and that won increases in naval expenditure and the fortification of Singapore. But in 1934 the Defence Requirements Committee reported to the Cabinet: 'We take Germany as the ultimate potential enemy against whom our long-range defensive policy must be directed.' They had concluded that whatever damage to imperial defence Japan might accomplish could not compare with the effect on Britain of a repetition of 1914. After 1934, directed chiefly by Baldwin and Eden, the government embarked on a policy of bringing Germany to terms, backed by the re-armament of all three services, but especially of the

The Coronation

RIGHT Intrepid sightseers in Piccadilly Circus.

FAR RIGHT The state coach passes thousands of school children along the Victoria Embankment.

BELOW A sea of umbrellas greeted the King and Queen on their return from the Abbey.

RIGHT The royal family in their coronation robes at Buckingham Palace after the ceremony.

OPPOSITE The scene in Westminster Abbey, May 24, 1937. The King has been crowned and the peers have put on their coronets. The Queen sits to the left, awaiting her crowning ceremony. Behind the array of gold plate stands Queen Mary with her grandchildren, Princess Elizabeth and Princess Margaret. Behind the King's throne stand the pages who carry his train. He sits on the Coronation chair first used at the coronation of Edward II in 1307.

RAF for which a whole series of new fighters was developed, together with the radar screen and a bomber strike force intended ultimately for use as a deterrent against further German aggression.

Unfortunately, this strategy was hampered by shortages of skilled manpower, technological difficulties and the competing claims of the civil budget. It had to be pushed through a House of Commons where the Labour Party resolutely opposed all measures of re-armament until 1938 and it had to be presented to a public wedded apparently to isolation and pacifism. Eleven

and a half million had pledged assent to most of the proposals in the Peace Ballot in 1934. Worse, for a government running up to a General Election, a long succession of by-elections in 1934–5, fought very largely on the issues of peace and re-armament, of which East Fulham was only the most notorious, revealed swings against the government of twenty to twenty-five per cent. By a dint of careful political education and electioneering, Baldwin was able to preserve his government's majority in November 1935, but the Cabinet remained unsure of how far they could carry support when the cost of the arms programme began to bite. All the time, the Dominions opposed any European policy likely to involve Britain in a war where their interests were not intimately concerned; and those interests also conflicted, because of internal weaknesses or factors like the wide-spread pro-German sympathy in South Africa. At the Imperial Conference in 1937, only New Zealand gave support to Britain's overall foreign policy.

The arguments in favour of a deterrent policy towards Germany were also discredited by the unpopularity of the link with France on which it rested, and by its apparent failure in the period up to 1937. Germany did not return to the League, the Disarmament Conference broke down, as did the French search for another Locarno agreement to cover Germany's eastern frontier. The short-lived *entente* of Britain, France and Italy, which had been achieved at Stresa in 1934, was broken by Mussolini's attack on Abyssinia, and the Anglo-French link itself barely survived mutual recriminations over the Anglo-German Naval Treaty and the Franco-Soviet Pact. Taking advantage of discord among the original Locarno partners, Hitler launched the occupation of the Rhineland in March 1936 and neither France nor Britain felt able to do more than pro-test. During the remainder of 1936, Hitler cautiously probed British intentions with a number of offers and promises, as he decided whether or not Britain was still a valuable 'natural ally', worthy of her own sphere of influence distinct from the future German hegemony over Europe. Meanwhile, Germany joined Japan in the AntiComintern pact and Italy in the Berlin-Rome Axis agreement.

As soon as Chamberlain became Prime Minister, the emphasis shifted from the search for *detente* based on deterrence to more direct appeasement of German grievances. The strategy of defence reflected the change: re-armament was concentrated on air defence rather than bombers and diverted from the army's expeditionary force. In January 1938, Chamberlain was ready to offer Germany extensive colonial territory in Central Africa; in March, the government first acquiesced in the *Anschluss*, or take-over of Austria, and then made a prolonged attempt to resolve the Czechoslovak dispute in Germany's favour before it led to European war. The success of the latter manœuvre destroyed the Franco-Soviet Pact, went far to shake the morale of France and ended in the partition of the only reasonably democratic state in Central Europe.

The road of appeasement, up to the time of Munich, can be justified from the British standpoint by reference to economic and military weakness in comparison with Germany, and by the strong disinclination of the government to face up to the possibility of a war in which Britain would be allied with Communist Russia. But it ignored the cardinal principle of earlier history that it was not in Britain's interest to allow a hostile power to hold Belgium and northern France; and it rested on assumptions about Germany's long-term aims which were seriously out of date. Within the Cabinet, Chamberlain's attempt to detach Italy from the Axis by making a separate agreement, and his masterful running of the Foreign Office, led to the resignation of Eden, the Foreign Secretary, and the formation of a small, like-minded inner Cabinet, with Lord Halifax in Eden's place.

The King, with vivid memories of the First World War, shared, like the overwhelming majority of people, Chamberlain's personal horror of war and air bombardment. Fears of what could happen to great cities in war, at least as potent as those inspired by thermo-nuclear war after 1950, were enhanced by bombing experience during the Spanish Civil War and by the Air Ministry's own statistics of likely casualties. On the other hand, while he knew little of grand strategy, the King loathed the aggressive philosophy of the dictator states. He believed it necessary to establish on whom the blame for war should rest and to that extent supported appeasement, but he also regretted the fall of supporters of a tougher line, such as Eden, and especially Lord Swinton, political architect of the striking power

of the air force: 'He will be a great loss to the country at this time.'

After the crisis of May 1938 when, on rather scanty evidence, the British considered that a mild rebuke to Hitler had fore-stalled an attack on Czechoslovakia, the King and Queen made a state visit to Paris. The time was unpropitious and recalled memories of George v's visit in April 1914, only four months before the last war. The immediate aim was to win French support for the mission to Prague led by Lord Runciman, to mediate between the Czech government and the Sudeten

German leaders. More generally, the British hoped to paper over the cracks in the Anglo-French *entente*. Daladier's Government, however, required something much more tangible in the way of guarantees before abandoning their own treaty with the Czechs.

The royal couple were given an enthusiastic welcome by the French crowds, belying the fears for security which had led the Paris police to surround them with a tight cordon. They were, after all, not merely young and charming but tangible proof that the *entente* survived, and a counter to the spreading apathy and pro-German leanings of many Frenchmen. The programme was crowded: at a banquet at the Elysée Palace, the King, in words obviously drafted by the Foreign Office, promised continued co-operation. Later he reviewed fifty thousand troops at Versailles. France still had the largest army in Western Europe but, for those with critical eyes, the vaunted and numerically enormous French air force was already obsolete in comparison with the latest German machines.

For much of the last month before Munich, the King was at Balmoral, where Chamberlain reported the failure of Runciman's mission and his own secret plan to visit Hitler. The King was kept as well informed as the Cabinet, that is, one step behind the real decisions on how to deal with Germany. But there was nothing he could do to affect events: his plan to write to Hitler, 'as one ex-serviceman to another' and beg him to spare Europe the disaster of war, was deflected by the Foreign Secretary. Chamberlain explained to him with considerable care, on 13 September, the reasons for his flight to Germany, claiming it as a last hope before the deadline for a German attack on Czechoslovakia. The King came south at once and over the next few days, until Chamberlain returned with a week to enforce conformity with German plans, concerned himself, very properly, that the world should know that the blame rested entirely with Germany.

On Chamberlain's second visit to Bad Godesberg, Hitler increased his price. The Sudeten areas were to be occupied immediately by German troops. Intensive and unsuccessful wrangling with France and the Czechs followed: Chamberlain was forced to give a verbal guarantee of support to Daladier on 26 September; Halifax and several ministers refused to

King George and President Lebrun drive past the town hall at Versailles with a large police escort.

accept the Godesberg *diktat;* and by the 28th war seemed
inevitable. A state of emergency was declared, the fleet mobil-
ised, gas masks issued and trenches dug across the royal parks.
The King yearned to do something, yet Chamberlain advised
against a national broadcast, and he was reduced to writing to
Queen Mary: 'It is all so worrying, this awful waiting for the
worst to happen.'

After Hitler accepted the invitation to resolve the dispute at
the Munich conference, relief in Britain found an enormous
tangible expression. The King sent Chamberlain 'heartfelt
congratulations' on the settlement and retired to Balmoral.
Yet deep political divisions remained: Duff Cooper, First Lord
of the Admiralty, resigned and sections of the Conservative
Party grouped together in opposition to Chamberlain. By-
elections in the autumn showed pronounced public antipathy
to the government's foreign policy and thus prevented discussion of a General Election. The fruits of Munich did not
exist. Chamberlain and Halifax tried to capitalise on the 'understanding' with Hitler, while at the same time wooing Mussolini.
They were rejected in both quarters. The safeguards agreed at

110

DOWNING ST. SERENADE

Daily Herald

Saturday, October 1, 1938.

...ning Street a great crowd waited to greet Mr. ...berlain when he returned home. They called for ...n and again, and when, in answer to their calls, he ...d at an upstairs window with Mrs. Chamberlain, they ...him with cries of " Speech, speech." Cabinet ...s forgot their dignity for the moment and cheered ...rest. Mr. Malcolm MacDonald and Mr. Geoffrey ...mbed to points of vantage on the gateposts of No. 10.

Members of the Cabinet crowded round Mr. and Mrs. Chamberlain on the steps of No. 10.

When he arrived at Heston Mr. Chamberlain read the Anglo-German Pact in front of the B.B.C. microphones.

STOP PRESS

BORDER FIRING

Machine-guns and rifles rattled furiously, and Very lights lit up countryside on Czech - German border at 1 a.m., says Reuter. Sudeten ou...ts cleared away barri-cades and were moving gingerly forward.

PRAGUE PROTEST

Czechoslovak Government communiqué accepting terms of settlement was issued in Prague l... night. Says Government "protests to world against Munich decision as being one-sided."—British United Press.

LS191
T417
E381

Printed by Odhams Press, Limited, and published on the "Daily Herald" (1929), Limited, London: Long Acre, W.C.2 and Manchester: Chester - street, Oldham - road, England. October 1, 1938.

A 545

Munich were disregarded and Germany arrogantly dismembered Czechoslovakia. Meanwhile, the government rearmed in a purely defensive sense and provided little for the army – not even tanks capable of operating in a European theatre of war.

The shock was all the greater when, in March 1939, following the Slovak secessionist crisis, German troops occupied Prague and the rest of Czechoslovakia. At last the government took stock, and feverishly set to work to create a defensive European alliance. Their hasty unco-ordinated diplomacy was only partly successful and the attempts to bring together the mutually mistrustful Poles and Russians failed, at least partly because of British distaste for the Communist regime. But the guarantee to Poland against German aggression committed Britain to fight for an objective in Eastern Europe, a reversal of centuries of cautious balance-of-power politics.

During the six months after Munich, the King loyally supported Chamberlain, who retained the enthusiasm of the great majority of the Commons and the newspapers. He was still not permitted to act on his own. Those who clamoured for the urgency of a Ministry of Supply or National Service had been defeated by the argument that these were undesirable except in wartime. The King proposed that he should broadcast about the voluntary scheme advocated by Chamberlain but this too was annulled on the somewhat absurd advice of the Bank of England that the gesture might create alarm and a slump on the Stock Exchange. In such a manner, Britain staggered into 1939.

After the break in appeasement in April and the further guarantees against Germany given to Greece, Romania, Holland and Denmark, the King felt happier. He wrote to Chamberlain, hinting that he approved the new policy: 'Although this blow to your courageous efforts on behalf of peace and understanding in Europe must, I am afraid, cause you deep distress, I am sure that your labours have been anything but wasted, for they can have left no doubt in the minds of ordinary people all over the world of your love of peace, and of our readiness to discuss with any nation whatever grievances they have.' Indication of his feelings, however correctly expressed, may be found also in his support of the war minister, Leslie

German-speaking Czechs give a warm welcome to the German soldiers occupying the Sudetenland by the terms of the Anglo-Franco-German pact at Munich.

Hore-Belisha, in December 1937, during the drive against the incompetence of the Army Council; and again, after Hore-Belisha's enforced resignation in January 1940, when the King remembered particularly that he had sought to introduce conscription early in 1939 as a preliminary to doubling the size of the Territorial reserves.

The King understood very well the need to be totally prepared if war broke out against the greatest industrial nation in Europe. And there was now a field in which he could be of great service. The disunity of the Dominions, clearly revealed at the Imperial Conference of 1937 and reiterated during the Czech crisis, had left the British government gravely worried

LEFT Princess
Elizabeth and Princess
Margaret in the park at
Windsor in 1941.

RIGHT Queen Elizabeth.

at the effect if and when Britain had to fight in defence of Poland or the others. The Commonwealth had been a major factor in the adoption of appeasement, but very little had been done to educate Dominion opinion to the reality of the European situation. For more than a decade, imperial defence had been a burden to Britain rather than a source of strength and one response had been to cut commitments, for example by giving Egypt independence while safeguarding the Suez Canal, and by the policy foreshadowed in the Government of India Act, in 1935. However, it was not possible in practice to coerce Dominion governments and there was a distinct possibility that Canada might stand by for fear of the effect on French Canadian opinion of a declaration of war, and that South Africa would split, as in 1914, into communities of English and Afrikaners. Australia, deep in self-imposed isolation, had voted against conscription in 1917. Nearer home, to conciliate Irish opinion in 1938, Britain had surrendered her rights to the use of ports and there was no certainty that, under the formula of 'external association', Eire would give any help at all.

As titular head of the Commonwealth, the King was superbly fitted to inject a note of unity in the last six months before war. Although the Canadian tour in May–June 1939 had been arranged as far back as 1937, it followed neatly on a similarly motivated lecture tour by Baldwin: 'Canada in my [Baldwin's] view is suffering from want of leadership … there is a nasty undercurrent of neutrality.' An equally important element was introduced after a cordial correspondence with President Roosevelt who invited the King and Queen to Washington and New York. The correct protocol here was vital if the United States was to be weaned away at all from the isolationism so obvious at the time of Munich. Halifax, the Foreign Secretary, could not accompany the King because the visit might then arouse old American fears of 'entangling alliances'. The gap was filled by the insistence of the Canadian Prime Minister, Mackenzie King, who had his own mark to make in the United States and had no intention 'that the King should cast him aside at the frontier like an old boot'. He was not the most congenial of travelling companions, but Lord Tweedsmuir, the Governor General, insisted, and since Roosevelt had no objection, the King agreed.

Fears for his security in the Atlantic, where the German pocket battleship *Deutschland* hovered off the coast of Spain, enforced an escort but the King did not want to deprive the fleet too much and the battle-cruiser *Repulse* turned back half way. The royal party was delayed by fog off the coast of Newfoundland, which gave the King the chance of a rest before the tour itself, an exhausting business involving several days and nights in the royal train. The results, however, justified any discomfort. One provincial premier told Sir Alan Lascelles, the King's private secretary, 'Any talk in the old country about Canada being isolationist after today is just nonsense.' Such judgments were valid: the tour swept away some of the accumulated mistrust about British intentions and reawakened dormant links of memory and sentiment. Tweedsmuir commented: 'The visit was a demonstration of our unity of spirit. ... I have always been deeply attached to the King and I realise now more than ever what a wonderful mixture he is of shrewdness, kindliness and humour. As for the Queen, she has a perfect genius for the right kind of publicity. ... The American correspondents were simply staggered; it was a wonderful example of what true democracy means, and a people's King.' The contrast between their direct simplicity and the barnstorming of American electioneering was particularly marked.

Long afterwards, Eleanor Roosevelt wrote: 'My husband invited them to Washington largely because, believing that we might all soon be engaged in a life and death struggle, in which Britain would be our first line of defence, he hoped that the visit would create a bond of friendship between the two countries.' A great barrier of isolationist opinion and recent history since the American rejection of the League of Nations in 1919 had to be surmounted first, but the King's visit proved to be, at the very least, a demonstration that Britain was not, as many west of the Alleghenies thought, governed by a decadent Euro-centric elite. In the high humidity of Washington, or at the World Fair in New York, escorted by that great showman Mayor Fiorello la Guardia, the royal couple repeated the euphoric success of the Canadian visit. At the end, they spent a short time in private talks at Hyde Park, Roosevelt's elegant mansion overlooking the Hudson River. The President was impressed with the King's grasp of affairs and allowed himself

to be optimistic about American policy towards Britain. Here were the germs of 'bases for destroyers' and perhaps also Lend-Lease. But he did not disguise the difficulties of putting such a policy into action. The conversation had most effect on George VI who asked Mackenzie King afterwards, 'Why don't *my* ministers talk to me as the President did tonight?' As an efficient envoy of his country, the King minuted in detail everything that Roosevelt had said.

In Britain, conscription had been brought in, after a lengthy Parliamentary battle, and in Europe Hitler had made his demands for Danzig. Months too late, Britain and France made a half-hearted attempt to enlist Soviet Russia as an ally but, unknown to them, Stalin pursued alternative negotiations with Germany which bore fruit in August in the non-aggression pact signed by Molotov and Ribbentrop. The effect on the West was disastrous although, ironically, the news fell hardest on the several Communist parties.

OPPOSITE The King and President Roosevelt drive through an excited crowd to the White House.

BELOW The King and Queen on the porch of Roosevelt's home, Hyde Park, New York. The President's wife sits to the left of the King and his mother to the right.

NATIONAL SERVICE
WE'VE GOT TO BE PREPARED!

MY REPLY TO GOEBBELS

The King's only part in the last months was to suggest the use of his cousin Prince Philip of Hesse, frequently a liaison between the dictators, as a messenger to convince Hitler that the British guarantee to Poland meant what it said. This looked too much like Hitler's own methods for his Cabinet; the instrument was also known to be too devious. Likewise, the Cabinet thought the King's suggestion of an overture to Japan, in the wake of the Russo-German pact, premature: British interests in the Far East were so finely balanced between excessive commitments and inadequate resources that they dared not risk a rebuff. Instead of being a mediator, the King visited Dartmouth and held his last memorable camp at Abergeldie.

At the end of August the storm broke. After all the manoeuvrings and the diplomatic warnings, Hitler ordered the assault on Poland. For a short while there were fears of another Munich, in the government's procrastination and the timid response of the Dominion High Commissioners in London. But the messages of support from the Commonwealth Prime Ministers left no doubt, this time, of their support. On 3 September, the King began a diary: 'At the outbreak of war in 1914, I was a midshipman, keeping the middle watch, somewhere in the North Sea. ... Today we are at war again and I am no longer a midshipman in the Royal Navy. ... Today, when the crisis is over, and the result of the breakdown of negotiations is war, the country is calm, firm and united behind its leaders, resolved to fight until liberty and justice are once again safe in the world.'

OPPOSITE Despite the build up of tension, shown by this poster on Charing Cross bridge, there seemed plenty of time to relax on Brighton Beach in August 1939. On 31 August only eighteen per cent of those surveyed expected a war.

5
War
1939-45

ON THE FIRST NIGHT OF WAR, George VI broadcast to the nation as he had not been able to do during the long twilight of peace. He set out the principles by which he judged the coming struggle, and simply and directly addressed every family in the British Commonwealth, 'as if I were able to cross your threshold and speak to you myself'. Britain was to fight in defence of liberty, peace, justice against 'the mere primitive doctrine that might is right. ... This is the ultimate issue that confronts us. For the sake of all that we ourselves hold dear, and of the world's order and peace, it is unthinkable that we should refuse to meet the challenge. ... To this high purpose, I now call my people at home and my peoples across the seas. I ask them to stand firm and united in this time of trial.'

The formal duties of the King in wartime are no greater than in peace: he is already supreme Commander of the forces. But the nature of a society's organisation in any desperate emergency, as well as the methods of its press and radio, focuses attention with peculiar clarity upon its leaders, whether generals, politicians or monarch. In the First World War, according to the country involved, George V, the Kaiser, Queen Marie of Romania and the King of the Belgians were portrayed heroically, and in the second, Queen Wilhelmina of the Netherlands and King Haakon of Norway, in exile. Equally, failure condemned King Leopold, who chose to stay in Belgium in 1940 rather than follow his government into exile, and the Regent Paul of Yugoslavia who suffered almost universal execration for betraying his country to the Germans.

George VI was well aware that he would be called to appear in a more demanding role than hitherto. In his own mind, as he had shown in the first of many broadcasts, his prime duty to the nation was to inspire unity and single-minded devotion to victory, cost what it might. He had known of the failure of French morale in 1917 and he realised that the enthusiasm of the volunteers in Britain in 1914 had concealed deep divisions which the course of the war enhanced. Strikes had not ceased, in spite of the agreement between government and unions, and the later reports of the Industrial Unrest Commissions had indicated working-class anger at war profiteering, unfair incidence of conscription and rising rents and food prices.

Thus it was not merely a sign of good public relations that he

PREVIOUS PAGES The King and Queen inspect the damage to Buckingham Palace after the fall of a bomb in September 1940.

was one of the first to be fitted with a gas mask at the time of Munich. In the last year before the war, and during it, he set himself to live with duty as if to embody the national will, knowing that, from his position, even simple acts would radiate outwards, influencing the way in which ordinary people thought and behaved. At the state opening of Parliament in 1939, he wore naval uniform; and one observer noticed both the Queen, in black velvet – 'I have never seen her so regal and beautiful' – and the contrast between 'this morning's quiet ceremonial and all the Nazi fanfare'.

One of the King's most important jobs in the war was to maintain morale in the badly-bombed districts.

Women at War

During the Second World War all women between eighteen and fifty years old had to register for essential war work. Among them was Princess Elizabeth, who joined the ATS. By 1942 over six million women were employed in industry or the services.

LEFT Factory workers making parachutes.
BELOW LEFT The ATS Dance Band.
RIGHT Searchlights manned by the ATS.
BELOW The Women's Land Army at harvest time.

The use of poison gas was one of the few expected horrors which did not emerge during the war.

From the start of the war, when he could reach out through the wireless to the great majority of the British people, George VI began to win a distinctive and deep affection, confirmed in his famous message at Christmas 1939 when he used lines from a poem by Marie Haskins 'The gate of the year' – 'Go out into the darkness and put your hand into the hand of God. That shall be to you better than a light and safer than a known way.' The winter of 1939–40 was grim and cold, with one and a half million still unemployed, and a grievous lack of political inspiration during the 'phoney war'. Rumours and despondency abounded, and one journalist wrote: 'Nearly everywhere I went during those early months, I heard the same remark, "The British people will win this war in spite of their government."' Loyal as he was to Chamberlain, from that association the King was already free.

His influence and power to reconcile disharmony were to be exercised in foreign policy and imperial affairs, among political leaders and in public. The Canadian tour in 1939 had been undertaken in order to emphasise the links with British destiny. In spite of the long-term failure of British governments to evoke a general Commonwealth foreign policy, the dissensions in September 1939 were less than had been feared. None of the Dominions joined in the guarantee to Poland in March 1939. Even six months later there was evidence that they favoured a search for a negotiated peace, similar to Munich; but after the British declaration of war on 3 September they followed suit. In Canada, although Mackenzie King did not summon Parliament until the 7th, the decision was unanimous. There were two exceptions – General Hertzog regarded a war fought ostensibly for Poland as none of South Africa's business, and the unhealed divisions between those of English and Boer descent broke wide open in a Parliamentary vote of sixty-seven to eighty which brought Smuts back to power. Hertzog resigned and during the next five years many Nationalist leaders were restrained for their pro-Nazi sympathies. Eire, firmly entrenched in the newly-won 'external association', had no intention of declaring war, and it was no reward for Chamberlain's appeasement of de Valera that the use of the Irish ports was denied the British fleet – a grave strategic weakness in the face of German submarines and surface raiders which Churchill had foreseen when the rights were surrendered in 1938.

The King was as concerned to counteract faint-heartedness or despondency about Britain's likely survival as he was that the Commonwealth should act together. Collaborationist sympathies were only too apparent in France and Belgium in 1939. So he took pains to receive Joseph Kennedy, the American Ambassador, who was known to be prophesying a British disaster (and later wrote a memoir entitled *Why Britain Slept*), and wrote him a caustic letter instructing him, clearly and pointedly, in the British case against Germany. The possibility of subversion by the 'fifth column' caused the King to insist on the need for stringency to Sir John Anderson, the Home Secretary; he was glad of the addition of regulation 18B to the Defence Regulations in May 1940, and the imprisonment under it of Oswald Mosley, nearly four hundred members of the British Union of Fascists, Captain Ramsey MP and other members of the pro-Nazi 'Link' organisation.

Overseas, he took what part he could in the difficult

diplomacy of 1939–40, trying to keep the neutral countries of south-eastern Europe from falling wholly into the Nazi orbit. In 1937 the Cabinet had discussed means to bolster up the nominally friendly states of Romania, Yugoslavia and Bulgaria against German economic expansion and later, in 1939, they had some success in creating a Mediterranean curtain, including Greece and Turkey. But all countries close to Russia were unbalanced by the German-Soviet Pact. The King's letters to King Boris of Bulgaria may have strengthened his morale but could do little to offset the need of the German war machine for the oil, grain and minerals of south-eastern Europe. King Boris held neutral for a time, in spite of the dissolution of Romania in 1940, but he signed the Axis pact in March 1941.

Bulgaria was not so vital an interest as Yugoslavia and Greece, whose royal leaders both succumbed. Prince Paul, Regent of Yugoslavia, was weak, indecisive and nearly at the end of his tenure of office. In a futile attempt to preserve the monarchy, he took the German desert offensive of 1941 as a sign that British power in the eastern Mediterranean was finished, and joined the Germans, ignoring George VI's many appeals. The King of Greece was less culpable: he had called on Britain for military aid against an Italian attack in October 1940, and George VI had been constrained to reply that Britain was fully extended in North Africa. It was hard for either Yugoslavia or Greece to take British survival on trust, with Italy and Germany so close; but General Simovič turned Prince Paul out, thus precipitating the German conquest of both countries which extended, in spite of British aid, to Crete. Another personal intervention, with General Orbay, head of the Turkish military mission seeking aid from Britain and France in September 1939, was insufficient to offset Russian pressure, and Turkey, though a recipient of the Allied guarantee, remained neutral. The King had better luck in Egypt, where he took a tough line with King Farouk, backing up the British Ambassador in a request that the Egyptian King appoint a firmly pro-Allied Cabinet.

In his letters to foreign royalty, the King showed a robust understanding and defence of Britain's interests. He gave very strong advice to King Leopold of Belgium to follow his government into exile, although he did not recriminate with him on the surrender of the Belgian army which left the British expeditionary force wide open to German encirclement. The existence of the Free French presented perhaps the most difficult exercise in diplomacy: it was almost impossible to deal with General de Gaulle, who single-mindedly arrogated the status of representative of all France, and ignored the existence of the Vichy regime or those in strategically important North Africa who seemed more accommodating to Allied aims. France's central African colonies supported de Gaulle and offered a long term base, but the British destruction of the French fleet at Oran in North Africa with much loss of life caused deep offence. In October 1940, George VI sent a personal appeal to Marshal Pétain, head of the government of Vichy France, not to collaborate with Germany but it had no success.

Answers to German peace overtures were easier to find. The British government rejected Hitler's call to negotiate after the German and Russian dismembering of Poland; and the King found no difficulty in rejecting offers to act as intermediaries made first by Queen Wilhelmina and King Leopold and later, in 1940, by the aged King Gustav of Sweden.

In the First World War, George V had seen his duty as 'not to inflict upon Ministers and Commanders his own view of policy or strategy but, with constant vigilance, to advise, to encourage and to warn'. George VI accepted this implicitly, in a supportive approach to his political and military leaders. At the outset, he hoped for a genuinely national government but although Churchill and Eden joined Chamberlain's reorganised Cabinet, the Liberal and Labour leaders, still alienated by pre-war disputes, refused. The King was loyal to Chamberlain and believed firmly that disunity should not be flaunted in public; hence, with Chamberlain's assent, he encouraged Attlee to mute Opposition criticism of the government's lack of urgency at the end of 1939. He was powerless, however, to do anything about the dismissal of the War Minister, Hore-Belisha, in January 1940. Hore-Belisha's insistence on conscription had angered Chamberlain, and his demands for making the Belgian frontier defensible ran counter to French assumptions that the Ardennes were impassable to large German armies; moreover Lord Gort and the BEF particularly resented his criticisms of lack of energy, knowing that he had always previously knuckled under to the Prime Minister, after a show of strength on behalf of the army.

Nevertheless the obscure circumstances of his dismissal encouraged speculation that the army was to remain undemocratic and the King was not wrong to conclude that it represented the first serious crack in Chamberlain's prestige.

Criticism of the government grew steadily in 1940; for not aiding Finland against Russia, for not attacking Germany in the West and, finally, after the German invasion of Norway, for the almost total disaster of the attempted British counter attack. On 7 and 8 May, in the crucial Commons debate, passion against Chamberlain's leadership erupted much more violently than against Asquith in 1916. There were famous speeches by Leo Amery and Lloyd George, and Chamberlain responded ominously by relying on his friends. The final vote, a nominal government victory by 281 to two hundred was in fact a declaration of no confidence, and after it was made plain that the Labour Party would not stomach him, Chamberlain accepted unwillingly that he must resign. He preferred Lord Halifax to Churchill as successor. Some Labour leaders, like Dalton, concurred. But the manœuvres were interrupted by the German invasions of France, Belgium and Holland, on 10 May, which added weight to the demands for Churchill.

George VI was completely loyal to Chamberlain while he remained Prime Minister. He deplored the fury of the Conservative opposition and his warm sympathy continued in their correspondence, until Chamberlain finally resigned from Churchill's Cabinet in September 1940. At the end, the King took the trouble to visit the dying man whom he had greatly respected; and he wrote of 'poor Neville Chamberlain, whose resignation as Prime Minister was hard for me to accept and whose untimely death has robbed me of an adviser and friend'. He would have liked Lord Halifax to succeed, and suggested that it might be possible for him to sit in the House of Commons (a foretaste of peerage renunciation); but Halifax was unwilling and Chamberlain recommended Churchill.

The King was impressed by their first meeting: Churchill 'was full of fire and determined to carry out the duties of Prime Minister'. Yet it was not, at first, a congenial appointment. Churchill's record since the middle of the First World War had been erratic. Frequently rebellious, capable of enormous misjudgments, over Ireland and India, he had also taken Edward

VIII's side and consistently opposed Baldwin and Chamberlain in the 1930s. On 11 May the King wrote in his diary: 'I cannot yet think of Winston as Prime Minister. ... I met Halifax in the garden and told him I was sorry not to have him.'

This lack of appreciation soon disappeared. Churchill proved able to enlist Labour and Liberals in the Cabinet and magnanimously found a place for Chamberlain. Halifax became Foreign Secretary, Attlee Lord Privy Seal and Ernest Bevin Minister of Labour and National Service. Less than six months was needed for the King to observe Churchill's virtues, his commanding presence, driving energy and gift of channelling his determination into words to capture the mind and hearts of the British people. Formal audiences between them were soon replaced by regular informal Tuesday lunches when the King listened enthralled to the tidal flow of Churchill's table talk. 'I could not have a better Prime Minister', he wrote in February 1941; and Churchill himself acknowledged 'the gracious intimacy with which I, as first minister, was treated, for which I suppose there has been no precedent since the days of Queen Anne and Marlborough during his years of power'.

Churchill's appointment as Prime Minister on 10 September, 1940, was a great relief to the country and to him: 'At last I had the authority to give directions over the whole scene. I felt as if I were walking with destiny . . .'

The apparent inertia of the Chamberlain government during the months of 'phoney war', and the Allies' inaction on the Western front of Germany seemed to indicate that they were waiting for fresh peace overtures. To some extent, the government's failure was one of public education, because the chief reason for not bombing the Ruhr was not, as Kingsley Wood, the Air Minister, told the Commons, that the munitions factories 'were private property', but that he feared retaliation on London. Nevertheless there were signs that American opinion believed that the British were playing games. Morale was undeniably low at home and it was hard to give a sense of urgency to the troops in France. Before the fall of the government, the King had therefore prepared a special broadcast for Empire Day on 24 May, calling for a day of national dedication and prayer. Coming as it did, after the German armies had poured through the Ardennes, with the French in retreat and the BEF already almost surrounded, there was a singular fitness in his dignified, solemn summons to a holy war.

During that legendary early June, as the navy, the merchantmen and the fleets of small craft took off 224,000 British and

133

111,000 French troops from Dunkirk, the King was witness to the upsurge of self-help which annihilated despair. On the final night of the evacuation he received the Allied commanders: 'They all told me that same story of heroism and devotion to duty of the troops.' Unable to sustain the weight of the German advance, French resistance collapsed and although the King dispatched a personal message to President Lebrun, this, like Churchill's famous proposal of unity, was mere whistling down the wind. As Mussolini, desperate not to lose the fruits of a victory he had not won, joined Hitler and as the British Navy sank the French fleet at Oran, the King wrote to Queen Mary, with splendid pride: 'Personally, I feel happier now that we have no allies to be polite to and to pamper.'

Since spirit ranks with military and economic strength in war, the experience of Dunkirk and the notion of solitary combat from an island fortress were tangible things, exemplified in Churchill's broadcasts and his great Commons speech, offering nothing but 'blood, sweat, toil and tears'. Yet without the weapons left in France and without allies, it is most likely that Britain would have fallen, had Hitler ordered the invasion, Operation Sea-Lion, in the autumn of 1940. The significance of the Battle of Britain lay not in the huge numerical losses of the Luftwaffe but in the change of mind of Hitler and the German High Command. The daylight raids were switched from ports, airfields and radar stations to undefended London; and the massive invasion never took place. The foresight behind the development of radar and the eight-gun fighter, and the sacrifice of more pilots than the country could well afford, paid off, allowing sufficient time and resources for air production and training to make good the deficiencies. Afterwards, Britain was safe from direct seaborne attack and the prospect of the Gestapo actually established in London.

The immediate cost, however, was paid by London. Desperately short of anti-aircraft defences, only partly covered by the fighter screen, the city lay open to daylight bombing. The government had prepared plans to evacuate the nexus of war command, but deemed it impossible for psychological reasons, and the royal family likewise refused to move out, unless the Germans were actually fighting in the suburbs. The absence of preparations was lamentable. Buckingham Palace lacked even a proper air raid shelter in 1940; but the King took to practising with a rifle in the gardens, to the polite dismay of Lord Halifax, to whom he had given permission to walk through on his way to the Foreign Office. The Brigade of Guards provided a personal bodyguard for the King and Queen, known as the Coates Mission, against the chance of a German Commando sortie, an exercise regarded with some scepticism by the two veteran monarchs in London, Queen Wilhelmina and King Haakon, who had escaped the real thing. But this amateurishness put the royal family on the same footing as other Londoners who, with no Anderson shelters yet at the bottom of their gardens, had to flee into underground stations or lie hopefully in street gutters as the bombs crashed down from August onwards.

Until then, the King had been needed where the Services were; at Scapa Flow or with the BEF in France, or at remote Home Guard stations and aerodromes during the Battle of Britain. After August 1940, he was needed in the cities. The battle of London was won not by action but by the negative virtues, the courage of resistance and resilience. As the East End was reduced steadily to rubble, with fires blazing day and night, water and gas mains broken, dismembered bodies in the shells of houses, the will to survive remained. Everyone who experienced the Blitz had his own story of humour or gallantry. Firemen and ARP wardens became heroes, whole devastated streets acquired a community spirit previously unknown. Among the people, the smoke, the upturned pavements, the King and Queen went, listening, comforting; simply by their presence heightening the consciousness that every bomb-shocked individual was part of a national whole in which even outrageous loss made sense. This feeling of sharing, attested by private letters as well as the Press, increased markedly after Buckingham Palace was twice bombed in September. The first bomb exploded under the King's study at night, when he was at Windsor, causing only superficial damage; but on the second occasion, the King and Queen were watching from a window when two bombs exploded in the courtyard outside. Both were severely shaken and lucky not to have been killed or maimed by the flying glass.

They suffered delayed shock, yet the Queen could say afterwards: 'I'm glad we've been bombed: it makes me feel I can look the East End in the face.' 'The destruction is so awful', she wrote to Queen Mary, 'and the people so wonderful – they *deserve* a better world.' In order to give some recognition of the many acts of personal heroism by civilian workers who could not qualify for the awards of gallantry in the field, the King now created the George Cross and the George Medal and directed that they should rank directly after the Victoria Cross.

Much more was demanded of them in 1941 as the Luftwaffe switched to night sorties. Pathfinders, flying on radar beams, learned to pinpoint targets with incendiaries for the following flights of heavy bombers. In the first of these raids, the centre of Coventry was flattened and the Cathedral destroyed. The King arrived almost before the fires had been extinguished or the six hundred dead removed, and with the Home Secretary, Herbert Morrison, walked all day among the wreckage of obliterated streets. The people, though shocked, were pathetically grateful. Something very important was also established: London, centre of resistance and government, had recognised that the regions had their own suffering, no less real to bear. All over Britain, in cinemas, the one warm place of wartime entertainment, newsreels proclaimed the message.

On 22 June 1941, delayed longer than Hitler wished, because of the conquest of Yugoslavia and Greece, the German army attacked Russia and in doing so committed a substantial part of German resources to prolonged conflict and eventual failure. Whatever the British version of past history, Russia now became an ally. After a year in which the only question had been – could Britain avoid defeat? – it became possible to ask – how long must Britain wait before she could strike back?

Since the collapse of France had ended the thirty-seven-year-old *entente*, only the United States could help. At the beginning of 1940, a visit by the American Secretary of State, Sumner Welles, had shown the King that Roosevelt had been over-optimistic in the talks at Hyde Park in 1939. Given the history of mutual conflict over naval disarmament, relations with Japan, and commercial interests in the Far East which had embittered Anglo-American relations in the 1930s, it was not surprising. A legacy in the USA of strong mistrust of British diplomacy and imperialism outlasted the war itself. Yet, as Roosevelt knew, there were common links between them,

The King with Herbert Morrison (left) and the Very Reverend R.T. Howard, among the ruins of Coventry Cathedral. On the night of November 14, 1940, five hundred aircraft had dropped 543 tons of explosive on the city. 'I was horrified at the sight of the centre of the town' wrote the King, . . . 'the people in the streets wondered where they were, nothing could be recognised.'

especially after 1937, the year in which Hitler first acknowledged the United States as his ultimate enemy. American commercial rivalry with Japan, and concern at the implications of the Anti-Comintern Pact between Germany and Japan was real enough. But more than inside understanding of international tensions, or the sympathies of the President for George vi and Churchill, was needed to bring America into the war. Possibly the majority of United States citizens preferred Britain to win but the overwhelming number, on any opinion poll, opposed belligerency.

For two years, until the Japanese attack on Pearl Harbour in December 1941, the most that could be gained was 'aid short of war', and at first even this proved to be a matter of hard bargaining. There were long delays over the Western Atlantic patrol, operating from British bases, which Roosevelt had proposed to the King in 1939. $37 million worth of arms were shipped out for cash payment, but in order to appease a hostile Congress, the transfer to the United States of bases on British territory in the Caribbean was required in return for fifty outdated destroyers – sufficient to tide over convoy escort until British shipyards got under way. At this point, the King took his own independent line. He had used fully his friendship with Roosevelt to maintain a regular correspondence, and he had made tactful suggestions, which were warmly reciprocated, about joint co-operation in post-war reconstruction. United States claims on the new bases in the West Indies, however, began to resemble the thin end of a wedge of economic imperialism. The Bermudan authorities appealed to him against 'the new conception of American hemispheric defence' and the King told his private secretary sternly: 'These islands are part of the British Colonial Empire and I am not going to see my West Indian subjects handed over to the US authorities.'

The presidential election fell due in 1940 and he was able whole-heartedly to congratulate Roosevelt on winning an unprecedented third term of office. Military aid, at least, would continue. Then Lord Lothian, the British Ambassador in Washington and a life-long advocate of Anglo-American co-operation, died suddenly. In choosing as his successor a skilled interpreter of Britain, Churchill thought first of Lloyd George, leader in the First World War, and secondly of Lord Halifax, who, though an aristocrat, had the necessary dignity and prestige, and whose transfer would also leave the Foreign Office free from Churchill's former rival and open to his own nominee. Halifax, who considered himself still in the running for the highest office, was reluctant to go. Aware of the need to steer him away from Parliamentary criticism, the King deftly undermined his objections – 'The post of my Ambassador in the USA was more important at the moment than the post of Foreign Secretary here.'

The signal gesture made by Roosevelt in welcoming Halifax

in person as he arrived by boat was reciprocated when the King received the new American Ambassador (replacing the un-lamented Kennedy) at Windsor station. These signified a pronounced amelioration: in March 1941, cash payments for war materials were replaced by the Lend-Lease arrangements, in spite of opposition in Congress and Senate. To secure delivery of supplies, US naval patrols began to report the movements of German surface raiders and submarines, and when, even after the sinking of *Bismarck*, these measures proved inadequate, Roosevelt pledged sufficient support to defend the convoys against attack. The United States was now only one step from actual hostilities, and in August 1941, after the German attack on Russia, Churchill and Roosevelt, two 'former naval persons', met and drafted the Atlantic Charter.

George VI had for long been urging such a meeting to the President's special envoy, Harry Hopkins, but he judged it right to warn Churchill of the tremendous wartime and post-war obligations inherent in the Charter. Barring American partici-pation in the war, who was to defeat Germany? Russia seemed likely to lose her own war. 'We should have to do it ourselves', he told the Chief Whip: 'The USA had deserted us after the Great War in Europe and might easily do so again if she does not come in and feel the effects.' Fresh from his encounter with Roosevelt, Churchill refused to be put off and, in the event, Congress amended the Neutrality Act, thus allowing a wider scope to American assistance.

In December 1941, in the wake of Roosevelt's warning to Japan not to encroach on American interests in south-east Asia and the Pacific, came the attack on Pearl Harbour. The American fleet was caught at anchor unawares and, as a result, the British were left wholly exposed in the Pacific. Two of the finest capital ships in the navy, the battlecruisers *Prince of Wales* and *Repulse* were sunk off the coast of Malaya and in quick succession Hong Kong and the great fortress of Singapore fell to the Japanese. In spite of the promise of ultimate victory sustained by American entry into the war, the British suffered seven long months of rout, being driven back through Burma to the Indian border, and in North Africa by Rommel to El Alamein, only sixty miles west of Alexandria.

Consequently, demands arose in the House of Commons for

During the war certain
artists were commissioned
by the government to
record the scenes and
atmosphere around them.
Henry Moore and John
Piper found their
inspiration in the bombing
raids of 1940–41:
RIGHT *The Ruined House of
Commons* by John Piper;
BELOW *Shelter Scene, Bunks
and Sleepers* by Henry
Moore.

a change of leadership. With the strain of war on two fronts, against Germany and Japan, Churchill's tenure of the Ministry of Defence as well as the premiership, was severely criticised. The King, as deeply loyal to Churchill as he had been to Chamberlain, supported him in his resolve to retain ultimate direction of the war effort, with all that that entailed. But he acknowledged shrewdly, after the ministerial changes of February 1942: 'The House of Commons wants Winston to lead them; but they don't like the way he treats them. He likes getting his own way with no interference from anybody and nobody will stand for that treatment in this country.' The depth of his anxiety showed through in one of their weekly luncheons when Churchill hinted that parts of India and Australia might fall to Japan. 'Can we stick together in the face of all this adversity?' the King wrote afterwards. 'We must somehow.'

He was not much heartened by an encounter with Molotov in May. To the dismay of the Foreign Office, Russia was seeking British recognition of the territory snatched from Poland and the Baltic States in 1939. The British responded with calculated mistrust. The Russian army, weakened by Stalin's purges in the late 1930s, had failed to defeat Finland in the winter war of 1939–40, and had not yet shown its capacity to roll back the Germans on the Eastern Front. Eden, the new Foreign Secretary, would go no further than a noncommittal twenty-year alliance.

Political unrest surged for the last time in the summer of 1942, as dissident Conservatives moved a vote of censure on the government. Real grievances needed to be vented, but the means chosen by the mover of the motion, Sir John Wardlaw-Milne, were ludicrous: he proposed as a remedy not only that the Ministry of Defence should be separated from the premiership but that the Duke of Gloucester should be made Commander-in-Chief. Only Aneurin Bevan, on the Opposition side, came out with credit, and the attacks on Churchill virtually ceased.

The same month saw a substantial change in the balance of the war, as the Red Army turned back the Germans, and the USA took the offensive in the Pacific islands. The Axis advance was checked and Hitler's long-term strategic aims nullified, although Germany was far from defeated economically or militarily. The British public in November 1942 watched eagerly in their newspapers the arrows marking Montgomery's long advance from El Alamein, and the progress of Operation Torch, after the Allied landings in French North Africa. The latter, however, worried the King because General Mark Clark, the American commander, seemed too keen to deal with Admiral Darlan and other French officers tainted with collaboration under the Vichy regime. Even after Darlan's assassination, the old question of the Free French Forces bedevilled negotiations, as de Gaulle and General Giraud contested for allied recognition.

The King was sympathetic towards de Gaulle, whose stubborn intransigence he respected as a heritage from another France which had nothing to do with 1940, and he tried to explain these reasons to Churchill before the meeting with Roosevelt which took place at Casablanca in January 1943. The most serious trouble, however, arose from lack of co-ordination and battle experience: the US armies suffered a grave defeat by Rommel at Kassarene on the Tunisian frontier in February. Churchill was ill with influenza at the time, so the King wrote him a letter, full of good sense, advocating a stronger role for Harold Macmillan, then British Minister at Allied Headquarters, and General Alexander, Commander-in-Chief of British forces in the Middle East. He wanted them to knock the heads of the French together, but more especially to work out with the American commanders a firm programme for Operation Husky – the invasion of Sicily. His thinking ran parallel to the conclusions of the Casablanca Conference on the political direction of the war, which resulted in the appointment of General Eisenhower as Allied Commander-in-Chief.

George VI's judgment was rarely at fault in the area where politics and strategy met. He occupied, by the middle of the war, a position of valued counsellor to his ministers, although of course he had no control over their decisions. Churchill had faith and confidence in him and sometimes tried to associate him with policy. At a dinner-party of the War Cabinet at No. 10 in July 1942, for example, Churchill mentioned the idea that he should visit North Africa, received the King's consent and held a Cabinet to confirm the decision straight away. The King often worried about the risks involved in Churchill's travels to

142

the USA and Moscow. So much hope and planning was invested in one man, that he needed advice on what to do if the Prime Minister were killed. Churchill's formal, indeed unique, advice was that he should send for Eden; later when both men went to the Yalta Conference, he nominated the Chancellor of the Exchequer, Sir John Anderson.

With the other Ministers, the King came less frequently into contact. He admired Eden's work and would spare neither him nor Anderson to take up the post of Viceroy of India in 1943, but Eden always kept strictly to his brief, and the King found it difficult to *discuss* foreign affairs as he did with Churchill. Attlee was always dry and correct, and there were few occasions to talk to Bevin or Morrison. The King regretted it, and complained to Eden early in 1941 that it was not made easy for him to meet the Labour Party leaders. About the same time, in a conversation with R. A. Butler, the King showed his concern that the junior Labour and Conservative ministers should work well together, and he asked pertinent questions about their accommodation in the House of Lords and Church House after the Commons chamber had been gutted by bombs.

He was trusted, in return, with the innermost secrets of the war. Only four people, Churchill, Lord Cherwell, the scientist Anderson and the King knew the full story of 'Tube Alloys' – the development of the atomic bomb. He set high store by security mindedness, always testing out sentry arrangements on his visits: and he was horrified, in August 1945, when the US Secretary of State, James Byrnes (on his way back from Moscow with President Truman), started to talk at lunch, in front of the waiters, about the imminent use of the bomb against Japan. He closed the conversation at once: 'I think we should discuss this interesting subject over our coffee.'

The King's awareness of good publicity often preceded his ministers'. When Lord Woolton was made Minister of Food in 1940, he saw at once how much depended on public acceptance of rationing regulations and advice; he visited the ministry and did all he could to make the civil servants feel that theirs was essential war work. Throughout the war, the King supported what Woolton called the 'kitchen front' and did not forget to praise those who got few thanks, such as the Women's Land Army, who worked long hours, cold and dirty, and were denied at the end of the war the resettlement grants made available to Civil Defence workers. (In 1951, when he invested Lady Denman, the Director of the Land Army, the King told her: 'We always thought that the Land girls were not well treated.') His sense of timing was equally good with particular events. Knowing of Smuts's troubles in South Africa, the King let him know that he would have liked to present his Field Marshal's baton in person, and when Smuts came to London in 1943, he was asked to preach to the royal family in St George's Chapel. In May 1943, when the Germans surrendered in North Africa, the King sent Churchill, who was then in Washington, an open telegram of congratulations, which led *The Times* to print an unusually effusive leader entitled 'King and Ministers'. And the royal family brought home the meaning of war privations in the kindest possible way to Mrs Roosevelt on her visit to London in October 1942, leaving her with impressions of mingled grandeur and simplicity, huge chilly bedrooms and rations eaten off gold and silver plate.

In June 1943, the King felt able to visit the Allied troops in North Africa – an event the Cabinet judged not only good for their morale and that of the French, but appropriate as a commendation of the newly reorganised structure of command. He reached Algiers by air, thinly disguised as 'General Lyon', having flown the whole way in one stage because of fog at Gibraltar. For two weeks he embarked on an exhausting review of the major units, stretched across hundreds of miles of desert. There were conferences with Generals Alexander, Montgomery and Wilson, and above all with Eisenhower; at one lunch he sat between de Gaulle and Giraud, though he failed to moderate their antagonism. At Bone he inspected the British First and Eighth Armies, at Oran, Mark Clark's US Fifth Army and in Libya the Fourth Indian Division. He was not afraid of plain speaking, in private, and commented with a certain chauvinism on some of the American divisions: 'They have at last realised that their troops are not fit and hard, so they are copying our battle schools and PT.' Afterwards, at his own wish and at some risk, he sailed to Malta, only sixty miles from the Italian forces in Sicily. Battle-scarred, psychologically exhausted after the incessant raids of 1941–2, Malta had survived everything and the King had already with an imaginative

OPPOSITE On board the cruiser HMS *Aurora*, the King sails into Grand Harbour, Valetta. He recorded: 'Every bastion and every viewpoint (were) lined with people who cheered as we entered. It was a very moving moment for me.'

gesture awarded the island the George Cross. He wished, how-ever, to pay personal tribute and show that he recognised the sacrifices of the population, worse than those of any other part of the Empire. His arrival inspired one of the most haunting images of the war: the slim figure of the King, in white naval uniform, on the bridge of the cruiser *Aurora*, waving, while half the population of the island stood on the great half-circle of Grand Harbour, Valletta.

Victories followed, thick and fast. Sicily fell, and the Allies landed in Italy. Mussolini was deposed and Marshal Badoglio sued secretly for peace in Lisbon. Although the Italian front settled into a hard, slow fight, several German divisions were tied down to hold what remained of Axis authority. Off Norway, *Tirpitz* was crippled, *Scharnhorst* sunk; and best of all, at Stalingrad, von Paulus surrendered with nearly a hundred thousand German troops. The King presented a sword of honour to the battered city whose spectacular defence had crippled the Nazi advance.

These were good omens for the Teheran Conference between Roosevelt, Stalin and Churchill at the end of Nov-ember 1943. Already, as the tide of war turned, the long-term interests of each nation were diverging. Stalin had insisted on the second front, tentatively agreed at Casablanca; Roosevelt wished to attack Germany in north-western Europe; but Churchill, unwilling to leave Stalin free in the East, preferred a Balkan offensive, to bring in Turkey as an ally, and to link up with the Russian armies. In 1943, a sufficient measure of agreement still existed between the three leaders for them to settle for an invasion of the north coast of France. General Smuts, however, believed that Churchill had been right in considering a Mediterranean front, 'the soft underbelly of the Axis', and, fearing a stalemate like 1916 in Flanders, he enlisted the King's support. The King was impressed: 'I agree with Smuts about this', he wrote in his diary. 'If you have a good thing, stick to it. Why start another front across the Channel? F.D.R. wants to give Marshall a good job here as C in C. The Russians did not want us in the Balkans. They would like to see us fighting in France, so as to have a free hand in Eastern Europe.' In his only substantive essay in advice on strategic matters, the King invited Churchill and Smuts to a discussion under his aegis. But any hope of the three great powers co-operating in a single front was dispelled by the Teheran Conference. Churchill did send to the Chiefs of Staff a letter from the King, advocating the conquest of Italy before Operation Overlord began, but although Rome was won on 4 June 1944, that advice, too, was disregarded. Preparations for the Overlord assault went ahead under General Eisenhower, the Supreme Commander, and the King busied himself in the first half of 1944 with visits to the troops stationed and training in Britain.

In the strange surroundings of a classroom at St Paul's School in London on 15 May 1944, the details of Overlord were explained to the King, the War Cabinet and the Chiefs of Staff. At the end of the briefing, quite unexpectedly, the King stepped onto the platform and delivered a brief, crisp message: 'This is the biggest combined operation ever thought out in the world. But it is much more than this: it is a combined operation of two countries, the United States and the British Empire. As I look around this audience of British and Americans, I can see that you have equally taken a part in its preparation. I wish you all success and with God's help you will succeed.'

Shortly after that valediction, Churchill gaily informed the King that he intended to watch the D-Day landings in person from one of the escort cruisers. To the horror of his private secretary, the King replied that he would go too. He was dissuaded from exposing himself to danger, but in spite of protests Churchill refused to budge. He was, as Baldwin once said of him, 'once more the subaltern of Hussars of '96'. In the end, when the civil servants had failed, the King had to threaten to drive down to Portsmouth and prevent him. Petulantly, the Prime Minister gave way.

Shunning a more ostentatious ceremony on the eve of the invasion, the King broadcast a call for prayer and the liberation of Europe. His style was now familiar to millions, mature, restrained and utterly sincere. Ten days after the landings, he visited Courcelles beachhead in Normandy, decorated soldiers for gallantry and watched the heavy guns bombarding far inland. In July, it was the turn of the half-forgotten army in Italy: 'Alex told me he was particularly glad I had come out just at this moment as the troops rather feared that their campaign had been put in the shade by the press, ever since the landings in Normandy.' In October, after the liberation of Paris and Brussels, he was able to review Montgomery's Twenty-First Army Group in Holland.

The relaxation which became possible in Britain was checked only a little by the waves of flying bombs, the VI and, in 1945, the V2. Many of the King's friends were killed when one exploded during a service in the Guards Chapel in Wellington Barracks; indeed, he was no stranger to personal grief because his younger brother, the Duke of Kent, had been killed on active service, flying in Scotland in 1942. But although the war in Europe was not over, the need to maintain the Home Guard had passed, and the King thanked hundreds of representatives at a march-past held in Hyde Park to mark their disbandment. Post-war reconstruction began to exercise the government and the planners: and again the King was in tune with his Ministers' mood. As early as 1940, he had written: 'Life will not be easy after the war and we shall all have to stick together to rebuild our towns and cities and make a new start in life.'

Meanwhile, the summit meetings culminated in the conference at Yalta in February 1945. The King was dubious about

BELOW Ten days after D-Day the King toured the invasion beaches.

RIGHT Churchill, Roosevelt and Stalin at the Yalta Conference, February 1945. Two months later Roosevelt died suddenly.

the result and gave a welcome only to the summons to a United Nations conference in San Francisco, to prepare a charter with which to replace the old League of Nations. He had long feared Russian aggrandisement in Eastern Europe, believing, as did many Conservatives in the 1930s, that it represented a greater long-term menace than National Socialism, and he remembered Chamberlain's profound mistrust of Communist intentions. With deep misgivings, he saw the obligations to Poland and the other allies of 1939 dissolved in the *real-politik* of Yalta, where Roosevelt conceded and Russia insisted on her own sphere of influence, unchallenged by the Western allies. 'Stalin', the King wrote in his diary, 'has put his name to some very important negotiations, together with those of two very modern and enlightened countries, and can he play fair? These negotiations are the foundations of the future peace of the world, and will they ever be ratified?'

Churchill had shared these doubts but he had been overborne by Roosevelt. Then in April 1945, Roosevelt died suddenly, leaving the question of whether Truman, unknown outside the

149

The Royal Family with Winston Churchill on the balcony of Buckingham Palace on VE Day.

United States, could ever fill his place. The conclusion of the war in Europe went badly for the British and Americans who, delayed in the Low Countries and the Rhine, met the Russian armies only on the Elbe, leaving eastern Germany and Berlin behind what was to become the Iron Curtain. But since Russia was still an ally, such calculations remained private. Mussolini was murdered by partisans, Hitler committed suicide in the bunker under the Chancellory and Germany capitulated unconditionally on 8 May. That day Churchill lunched with the King and quietly, emotionally, they congratulated each other. Outside, the streets were full, not of ecstatic crowds as in November 1918, but of people soberly, rather wearily, relieved and grateful to be alive. The royal family appeared eight times on the balcony of Buckingham Palace during the evening, in front of the Mall filled solidly down to Admiralty Arch; and afterwards the King let the Princesses go out, escorted by a party of young officers, to mingle in the lights. Princess Elizabeth was nineteen, Princess Margaret fifteen: 'Poor darlings,' he wrote, 'they have never had any fun yet.'

For the British, VE day was the end of the war. The struggle in the Pacific was remote, except for those with relations fighting in Burma or prisoners of the Japanese. Few people had appreciated that the US naval action at Midway was one of the decisive battles of the war. So, physically and mentally tired, the King rested at Windsor and summed up his personal record: 'We have only tried to do our duty during these five and a half years.'

From the record of his diaries, George VI had an even keener sense of duty in wartime than his father, and he was never satisfied that he had done enough. By any standards, he was successful in what he had tried to do. Much of the advice which he gave to Churchill and his government was not acted on, but this does not detract from the fact that, freer than his Ministers from the need for political compromise, he could stand firm in defence of what he believed were British interests, impartially against Russia or the United States. In the public sphere, his work is less easy to assess without inviting a deluge of sentimental memories. It is impossible to quantify the effect of any single personality on the course of a country's history and no poll exists to show what the average man – if he existed – thought of the King between 1939 and 1945. Most likely, he took for granted the dedication of national leaders and became accustomed to the simple honesty of George VI's style of speech. Sir Robert Menzies, the Australian Prime Minister, used to tell a story after his visit to London in 1941, of how an onlooker, near a bombed site in London, had shouted 'Thank God for a good King' – to which the King replied 'Thank God for a good people.' In this manner he was portrayed, in the papers and the newsreels, and for once the man and the reputation were the same. Among a hundred impressions, one retrospect is enough, from an author who was only five in 1939: 'I have been trying to think back to the war and how one felt about him, and all I keep remembering is that it was such a proper and decent thing to have a King of our country; and that the Germans had no one to be really loyal to, so in my childish mind I thought that they didn't have the same incentive to win the war.'

6
The New
Order
1945-51

DURING THE MONTHS AFTER VE DAY, Britain experienced a curious hiatus and a widespread feeling of anticlimax and unreality. The war was over, yet the peace had not begun. Numbers of civil defence workers could not get out of the habit of reporting for wartime duties. A jaded war-weariness pervaded everything and a reluctance to face the shortages and austerity which were universally, and correctly, predicted. Like moles exposed to sunlight, people hankered for the tunnel they had known. Ahead loomed vague unpleasantnesses, a balance of payments crisis, huge external debts and a world situation vastly different from that which Britain had set out to preserve by the declaration of war in 1939.

The mood was broken sharply by the use of the atomic bomb on Hiroshima, where seventy thousand died, and on Nagasaki. A fresh spurt of rejoicing followed. The King's broadcast awakened recently buried memories: 'The war is over. You know, I think, that those four words have for the Queen and myself the same significance, simple yet immense, that they have for you. ... From the bottom of my heart, I thank my people for all they have done, not only for themselves but for mankind.'

But the main event was undoubtedly the General Election. It had been obvious that the party truce was not likely to outlast the war. No General Election had been held since 1935 and the war-time by-elections had not been contested between Conservatives and Labour, so that the Parliament still sitting was largely unrepresentative. In October 1944, Churchill declared that it would be wrong to continue after the defeat of Germany. In party terms also, there was nothing of common interest to hold the coalition together as Lloyd George had done with Liberals and Conservatives after 1918. Ideological differences appeared every time reconstruction and post-war policy were discussed. Labour ministers resented Churchill's half-heartedness, for example, in not readily accepting the Beveridge Report in 1943 and voted as a party against him in the Commons. By 1945, Attlee was under pressure to end the coalition in the summer; on the other side, Lord Beaverbrook and Brendan Bracken were urging Churchill to ask the King for a dissolution quickly in order to ride to power on a flood tide of emotion at the victory in Europe.

PREVIOUS PAGES An ex-serviceman tries on his free 'de-mob' suit.

154

Churchill proposed instead to carry on the coalition until the defeat of Japan – an event not expected for eighteen months. Bevin and Attlee, unsure of a Labour victory, were inclined to agree. Neither of them knew of the atomic bomb and the case for first winding up the war and bringing the troops home seemed strong. But the Labour Party Conference at Blackpool demanded dissociation as soon as possible and Attlee was constrained to reply that he could go on no longer than October 1945. Judging that six months of caretaker government would be an advertisement of British weakness, Churchill decided to go for an election in July.

Labour and Liberal ministers resigned on 23 May, giving the King the chance to thank them personally for their work during the war. At Balmoral, seeking rest and tranquillity, he speculated on the likely results: 'The outcome is uncertain as no party may

The devastation of Nagasaki after the explosion of the atom bomb.

secure a clear working majority, which will make things difficult for any government, to try and deal with the USA, Russia and France, let alone setting up a government in Germany, and with all the problems of demobilization and housing at home.' He was less well informed of public opinion than the troops or civilian workers, who sensed a strong undercurrent in Labour's favour, or Smuts, who predicted a swing to the left and a situation in which the King would have to exercise a stabilising influence.

The tone of the campaign went far to discredit the Conservatives. Churchill's notorious speech, in which he claimed that Socialism could be established only by the use of Gestapo methods, lost him much public goodwill. The attempt to fight under his reputation alone – 'Send him back to finish the job' – backfired. In sharp contrast to 1918, when the pre-war world had seemed desirable to restore, no one wanted to return to the predominantly Conservative years of government, the poverty and unemployment of half Britain in the 1930s. Even before 1945, there had been clear signs of a change in the electorate: Sir Richard Acland's left-wing Commonwealth Party won three seats at by-elections; dissemination of the Beveridge Report

Churchill eats a roadside lunch during the 1945 election campaign. 'I am worried about this damned election' he said. 'I have no message for them now.'

and reconstruction plans woke an avid response, especially among the Forces, and all reports of public opinion indicated an extremely high level of post-war demand, not in the traditional Conservative sphere of foreign affairs, but for full employment and social security. The result, on 26 July, proved to be the greatest landslide since 1906: Labour, 393; Conservatives, 213; Liberals, 12; Independents, 22.

Churchill's message, conceding victory, reached Attlee and his colleagues at Transport House. At once the ambitious Morrison claimed that the Parliamentary Labour Party must re-elect its leader. Attlee squashed this attempt to limit his authority: 'If you're invited by the King to form a government, you don't say you can't reply for forty-eight hours!' So, as Churchill's chauffeured limousine left the Palace, Mrs Attlee drove her husband into the courtyard in their old Standard Ten. The waiting crowds cheered: 'We want Attlee' and the King observed 'Mr A looked *very* surprised!'

During the interview, the King took the responsibility for one far-reaching piece of advice. In response to Attlee's preliminary choice of Dalton as Foreign Secretary, he disagreed. His own suggestion was Ernest Bevin, for whose work as Minister of Labour he had the greatest respect. It was vital, he believed, to have the best man possible to control external relations. The King may have feared that because Labour Ministers had been almost wholly preoccupied with home affairs in the war, they might ignore what to him was the overriding danger of Russian territorial expansion. He was probably also aware of Dalton's sympathy with Russia and the fact that Morrison aspired to the Foreign Office. Moreover, the appointment had to be made at once, so that the Foreign Secretary could accompany Attlee to the Potsdam Conference, where Truman and Stalin were awaiting the new British representatives. How much the King's advice counted for is uncertain: foreign affairs are traditionally an area in which the monarch's advice has particular weight. Attlee later denied any royal influence, but he could hardly do otherwise, and he did persuade Bevin to abandon his preference for the Exchequer, risking both his disappointment and that of Dalton. The result, in Europe and the Middle East, was of enormous significance for the future of Britain.

The King recorded his melancholy at Churchill's departure:

'I saw Winston at 7 pm and it was a very sad meeting. I told him I thought the people were very ungrateful after the way they had been led in the war. He was very calm and said that with the majority the Socialists had got over the other parties, and with careful management, they could remain in power for years.'

A spectacular programme of legislation was set out in the King's speech to Parliament on 16 August 1945. Nationalisation of the mines, of the Bank of England, road and rail transport, gas and electricity, and the creation of a National Health Service were there to fulfil the Labour Party's pre-war pledges; controls over economic development were to be retained and perhaps increased to prevent the relapse into a private enterprise free-for-all which had marred recovery after 1918; and beyond this, the speech forecast a firm commitment to social revolution by changes in educational opportunity and the transfer of wealth.

Ernest Bevin presiding at the Paris Peace Conference in 1946.

These were of course the government's words not the King's. His own conception of reconstruction and reform was based less on ideology than liberal sympathies, not unlike those of Beveridge. As early as 1941, as his correspondence with Roosevelt shows, he had been preoccupied with questions of resources, financial stability and monetary reform after the war. With great foresight, he had urged the Foreign Office to impress on the United States the need for a joint declaration, welcoming a future voluntary European federation and British support for it. The response then had been cautious, fearful of committing Britain to more than a future government wanted or could do; but the King's wishes were at least met by the work of the ministerial committee on reconstruction which led on to the Beveridge Report. Lord Woolton recounted the story of how in 1943 his wife told the King of his efforts to get water supply extended to houses in the remote countryside and the poorer parts of towns, where for generations the occupants had to trudge to a common pump. 'It isn't enough', the King replied. 'What you want is a plug in every house' – 'and with that wave of his arm, expressed an ideal in public health which we have not yet accomplished'.

Some of his sentiments, however, were less acceptable to a Labour government. The King hoped for the continuation

of compulsory military service after the war as the basis of national defence and he had firm ideas about the appearance of the forces. He disliked battle dress: 'I want the Army to be popular and for soldiers to have a uniform which they will be proud of', he wrote. 'All questions relating to uniform must come before me before any alterations to it are discussed, let alone settled.'

With his insistence on correct turn-out (he had rebuked King Peter of Yugoslavia during the war for wearing a gold watch-chain with the uniform of the Yugoslav royal air force), he resembled his father and grandfather, and he was quite prepared to cross swords with Attlee on the subject. 'We must *all* have new clothes, my family is down to the lowest ebb', he replied caustically, in August 1945, when told that all available suits were to go to demobilised soldiers. But on the main issues, of priority in housing, building materials, demobilisation, he was in complete agreement.

The future handling of foreign affairs worried George VI to whom Mountbatten's hint was welcome: 'You will find that your position will be greatly strengthened since you are now the old experienced campaigner on whom a new and inexperienced government will lean for advice and guidance.' But there was no need for concern. In spite of the hiatus at the Potsdam Conference, where Stalin and Truman had begun negotiations with Churchill, and in spite of Molotov's expressed mistrust at negotiating with the representatives of a bourgeois Socialist party, Attlee and Bevin achieved as much – or as little – as the Conservatives could have done from their position of relative weakness.

A natural disinclination to be too closely associated with royalty showed itself in the relations between Labour Ministers and George VI during the first year. The King, after all, was not a Socialist and tended to disapprove of change which was not gradual and evolutionary. The omens for their co-operation were ambiguous. Over the previous forty years, the Labour Party had, under MacDonald, settled into the pattern of Parliamentary politics and become one half of the two-party system. On the other hand, Labour was a federal, often divided organism. The cry 'Socialism now' had been heard as early as 1909 when Victor Grayson attempted to draw the ILP away from Parliamentary politics. In the late 1920s a fierce battle had been fought to decide whether the Party Conference or a future Labour Cabinet should decide policy; and in 1932 the ILP had disaffiliated, seeking a revolutionary future outside Parliament altogether. Although both that and the United Front with the Communists failed, left-wing politicians imprinted an extremist message on some Labour Party thinking in the 1930s. Harold Laski's *Democracy in Crisis* proclaimed that a future Labour Government would have to govern by decree, and Stafford Cripps, the founder of the Socialist League, went further, advocating emergency powers to prevent a 'capitalist dictatorship'.

Cripps was in the government in 1945, having been a respectable if wayward member of the War Cabinet; Laski had become Chairman of the Labour Party; and the Cabinet, whose average age was over sixty, looked anything but volatile. Yet the King felt deeply the need to work within and preserve the traditional forms of government and he watched with care in case his ministers, in their urge to promote rapid change, contradicted his understanding of the constitution. The only disagreement of any consequence occurred over the Supplies and Services Bill, introduced in 1947 to extend and supplement the Transitional Powers Act of 1945. The Bill was intended to give cover for increased controls and restrictions in that crisis year but the Conservative Opposition stigmatised it as 'a blank cheque for totalitarian government'. Attlee underrated the significance of the attack when – perhaps disingenuously – he told the King, before the summer holiday at Balmoral, that it was only a minor piece of legislation. In Scotland the King discovered more from the Press and wrote anxiously to Queen Mary: 'The government have got themselves into a nasty mess over that Bill, which I was told was not a serious one when it was first thought of.' He sent a reproachful letter to Attlee requesting a full explanation, but from that master of the dry phrase elicited only a long, prosaic recital, pointing out the exaggerated nature of the Tory allegations. The Parliamentary storms subsided and Labour did not rule by decree; and Attlee was able to get what he wanted without succumbing to the King's advice.

The King preserved an impeccably correct attitude toward

government policy and showed his fundamental distrust of Socialist ideology only in such things as the way in which, over this Bill, he tended too easily to accept Churchill's rhetoric in place of political analysis. According to Channon, those Labour ministers who served in the Royal Household disapproved of the attitudes he betrayed in private, but this argues an excessive sensibility on their part. George VI could hardly have done otherwise than deplore the effect of estate duties and taxation on his friends and the society in which he had been brought up. In February 1948, when he made Vita Sackville-West a Companion of Honour, he asked after her family's great house, Knole, and on being told that it had been given to the National Trust, 'raised his hands in despair. "Everything is going nowadays. Before long, I shall also have to go." '

In the event, neither the monarchy nor the great families were doomed; the whole apparatus of redistributive taxation achieved only a small shift in the balance of wealth by 1951. Very little republican sentiment clouded the future of the monarchy, and after his record in the war there could be none of the recriminations visited, for example, on the ill-fated Kings, Leopold of the Belgians and Victor Emmanuel of Italy. The censure of Labour MPs, where it existed, was confined to what were judged extravagances in the Civil List or the revenues of the royal estates. The monarchy was too useful to question in the way that the continued existence of the House of Lords was questioned. It was also intensely popular, perhaps more so than before the war. The alternative of a presidency was scarcely even argued. But its value rested very largely on the relationship between the King, as a man, and his ministers.

At first, dismayed at losing the trusted Churchill in the face of a world crisis which bore with peculiar intensity on Britain, the King found it hard to get to know or to unbend to them. 'My new government is not too easy and the people are rather difficult to talk to', he wrote to the Duke of Gloucester. 'Bevin is very good and tells me everything that is going on. The others are still learning how to run their departments, and their efforts have not made life any easier so far. Food, clothes and fuel are the main topics of conversation with us all.' Attlee's conversation tended to be crisp and unemotional, neatly pinpointing the centre of an argument, like the celebrated phrases of the Duke of Wellington, and there were some long silences during their audiences. Discussion between them became easier with time, although Attlee preferred not to respond when the King delivered an implicit rebuke. 'I told Attlee that he must give the people here some confidence that the government was not going to stifle all private enterprise. Everyone wanted to help in rehabilitating the country but they were not allowed to.'

Attlee's gifts lay in the field of Cabinet politics rather than in public inspiration. Neither an ideologue nor a publicist, he maintained the balance between divergent personalities and ensured that, as far as the restrictions of time, health and the Parliamentary system allowed, the Labour programme should go through. The King missed, in him, the frankness of Bevin, who was at pains to show his mastery of foreign affairs, and who delighted him by his firmness towards Russia. Even Aneurin Bevan, feared as a wild man of the left, charmed the King by discovering a common frailty in their youthful stammers. Attlee may have been grateful for the advice the King gave about the difficulties of the Parliamentary timetable and the drafting of Bills which stood in the way of nationalisation legislation, but it is more likely that, beset by demands to override the restraints, he ignored it. He certainly did not confide in the King as Churchill had sometimes done when serious trouble was imminent. This gave some offence. Conscious of his length of experience, George VI wrote early in the disastrous year 1947, 'I have asked Mr Attlee three times now if he is not worried by the domestic situation in this country, but he won't tell me he is, when I feel he is. I know I am worried.' His concern, as he told a friend, was 'to warn them that they were going too fast in their legislation and were offending every class of people who were ready to help them if they were asked to, but were swept aside by regulations etc'. The King was convinced that he knew the mood of the country at least as well as his government, and that the people would no longer rally to calls for sacrifice as they had done during the war. The exceptionally harsh winter of 1946–7 went some way to prove him right.

During the six years of Attlee's premiership, a mutual trust and respect did develop between them, which could be seen for example, in the cordial correspondence preceding Attlee's visit to the United States in December 1950 to persuade Truman

OPPOSITE The King with Mr Attlee. Their relationship was not easy.

162

not to extend the Korean war nor to drop the atom bomb. The King's encouragement and good wishes obviously touched Attlee; but it was still noticeable that he had not been able to find time to warn the King in person, of his journey.

George VI's hard work on state papers and the thought he put into his advice impressed the departmental ministers. Anxious to preserve complete impartiality, he did not even dictate a record of his audiences with them but wrote it only in his diary (to the dismay of his private secretary who felt inadequately employed). Herbert Morrison, the Home Secretary, found that he always read carefully the reports of murder trials before discussing the exercise of the death penalty; and he primed himself on questions of the day before any audience, knowing the King's habit of firing penetrating questions to keep him on his toes.

Terms appropriate to the modern exchanges between King and ministers were evolved in these years, answering to a great extent the questions raised before the war about the sovereign's implicit links with one sector of society rather than another. They involved greater formality and a greater distance between them, as individuals, and reflected, naturally, the true political balance. The real friendliness of his first three Prime Ministers, Baldwin, Chamberlain and Churchill, may have disguised the limits of the Crown's influence, just as the extent to which the King absorbed their ideas and followed their policies encouraged him to think that they listened, perhaps more than they did.

The Labour government's legislation was based on party planning dating from 1918 and on the manifestos of the inter-war years, but in spite of the long evolution of the nationalisation programme, a great deal of detailed planning was still necessary; the Beveridge Report, basically liberal in its assumptions, could be only an introduction to the welfare schemes and to the National Health Service which Aneurin Bevan had to draft. The government inherited and put into operation the Family Allowances Act and R. A. Butler's all-party Education Act of 1944; and the main Parliamentary battles developed over nationalisation. The Bank of England fell easily – for fifteen years it had been virtually an offshoot of government – and the railways and mines, which the Coalition Government had nearly nationalised in 1919, proved no more resistant than the gas and electricity industries. Road transport and, above all, iron and steel, were the contentious items. The latter could not be said to be inefficient, and concern for its productive capacity was reflected across the whole of manufacturing industry. Yet an integrated transport and public utility system, and a control over the 'commanding heights of the economy' were vital for the government. Because the Steel Bill was introduced only late in 1948 and faced not only opposition in the Commons but rejection in the Lords, the government was constrained to alter the Parliament Act of 1911, reducing the delaying power of the upper house to one year. Even then, the Bill was not passed until shortly before the 1950 election and the industry was restored to the private sphere by the Conservatives after 1951.

For the rest, the opposition was largely token, designed to delay and embarrass the government. Conservative administrations had, after all, introduced state capitalism in the inter-war years, via the BBC, Central Electricity Board and BOAC. The new nationalised industries looked much like the old, with the same class of managers on the boards; no echo there of the once powerful cry of workers' control, nor even workers' participation. Meanwhile, demobilisation and reconversion to peacetime production went ahead rapidly and, given the strict controls of 1945, far more smoothly than in 1918, accompanied by a frenetic and remarkably successful drive to recapture lost export markets. Although production for the home market could not possibly meet the pent-up demand, fuelled by full employment, for consumer goods and houses (of which four million had been damaged or destroyed), until the mid-term of the government, around 1947, this did not seriously entrench on its popularity or on the public's assessment of its success.

The overriding problem was the external financial position. On 14 August 1945, Maynard Keynes presented a Treasury minute in which he predicted a 'financial Dunkirk' unless American aid continued. On VJ Day, 17 August, the existing Lend-Lease arrangements ceased; and Britain had to face up to the implications of an uncovered external debt of £3,355 million (of which £2,723 million lay within the sterling area), an 'invisible' income reduced by more than half because of the sale of £4,200 million overseas assets and investments, a huge internal debt, a £300 million deficit on the balance of payments for 1946 and a reduction of exports to a mere forty per cent of the 1938 total. Credit factors did exist: with full employment and rapid demobilisation, a large reservoir of labour was available for export industries; and the new industries themselves had been given decisive superiority over the old, completing the twentieth-century industrial revolution. But these were long-term factors and insufficient to offset the effects of American competition.

Keynes himself had already helped to negotiate the Bretton Woods Agreement in 1944 which was to lead to major reforms in world monetary policy, the World Bank and the International Monetary Fund. The value of these institutions to Britain, however, was diminished by the problem of sterling balances and the heavily over-valued parity of the pound against the dollar. Keynes and Halifax embarked on fresh negotiations in Washington in September 1945, but they encountered American hostility to Britain's continued imperial links, especially tariff preferences, suspicions of the motives behind the Labour government's plea for a loan, and a marked reluctance to fund Britain on any terms other than a strictly business footing. The delegation was successful in raising $4,000 million at the modest rate of two per cent interest, but on the crippling condition that sterling must be made freely convertible into dollars after twelve months. The terms were harsh, even nonsensical, for the British economy could not and did not, in practice, sustain them. Convertibility was abandoned in 1947 after one disastrous month's loss of $700 million. But the Labour Government had no choice but to accept.

1947 proved to be the watershed: a year in which scarcely anything went right. It opened with the worst winter in living memory and a coal shortage, blamed by the public, with only slight justification, on the government and the Minister of Fuel and Power. Bread was rationed; income and indirect taxes were raised; and the hardly-won dollar credits were eroded, as prices rose in the United States, and virtually exhausted by the end of the summer. The surge in exports was inadequate to offset a long-term shift in the terms of trade which had been at

166

work to Britain's disadvantage since the 1930s. Much of this was beyond the capacity of any government to affect, whatever its emergency powers. But criticism mounted rapidly in 1947 and although the Labour Party was not necessarily discredited, many of its most ardent supporters confessed to disillusionment. The Cabinet seemed to have run out of plans, to have abandoned the great social revolution for temporary expedients, and to have lost the buoyant energy of its first two years of office.

People queuing during the coal crisis to collect coke from the Bow Common Lane Gasworks, Poplar.

The King wrote an exaggeratedly pessimistic letter from Balmoral in September: 'I do wish one could see a glimmer of a bright spot anywhere in world affairs. Never in the whole history of mankind have things looked gloomier than they do now, and one feels so powerless to do anything to help' – exaggerated, because the United States government had already intervened, finding it necessary to stimulate European recovery or see world trade, by which the USA also lived, collapse. On 5 June 1947, in his famous speech at Harvard, General George Marshall outlined the terms of a European recovery programme. Marshall Aid followed, handed out with a generosity as amazing as the earlier bargaining had been hard.

The offer was seized on by Bevin, the Foreign Secretary, and for a brief period in 1948, British recovery advanced at a deceptive speed. But nothing had really changed; Marshall Aid only prevented the crisis from coming earlier. 1949 witnessed a

167

spiral of rising costs, prices and wage demands and a run-away rise in the dollar deficit. Stafford Cripps and Bevin made a fruitless pilgrimage to Washington and Ottawa, in search of support, while the King, who understood the dimensions of the problem, minuted 'If the talks do not go well, we may have a general election this year. What I fear is another 1931 crisis.' In September, the government conceded the need to devalue and the parity of the pound was cut dramatically from $4.03 to $2.80, accompanied by a renewed onslaught of austerity.

A later generation, grown accustomed to devaluation as a deliberate act of policy, has lost the sense of national humiliation which cursed the unfortunate Labour Governments of 1931 and 1949 for failing to sustain the value of the pound. At the time, it seemed like another Singapore. Devaluation was at least two years overdue but it helped. So did the widening of Marshall Aid, and the King was able to welcome, in his Christmas broadcast of 1949, the 'imagination and sympathy' shown by the American government. Nevertheless, the government's stock slumped. Its electoral record was excellent: not a single by-election had been lost since 1945; but Attlee judged it wise not to run the risk of going the full five years and he took the unusual course of a February election.

Apparent loss of purpose since 1947, the continued stringency of rationing and controls, the dissolution of the Empire and Britain's diminished status abroad were all hostages in the hands of a Conservative Opposition which had been revived and largely reborn during the previous five years. Labour's enormous majority vanished, leaving stalemate between the parties: Labour, 315; Conservatives, 298; Liberals, 9. Attlee had such a small overall majority that any death or illness among Labour MPs could have been disastrous; a situation in which an intelligent Opposition, staffed with gifted obstructionists, could literally wear the government down and out. Necessary as it was to see the Steel Bill through, Attlee's decision to continue in office with an elderly Cabinet and a distinct lack of popular mandate was not easy.

For the first time in his reign, the King had to prepare for a possible constitutional dilemma. Precedents existed for him to look to the Conservatives to form a government, without a General Election, if Attlee were to ask for a dissolution, and if the Parliament still appeared representative and vigorous. With the ambiguous and, in retrospect, mistaken decision of the Canadian Governor-General Lord Byng in 1926 in front of them, however, the King's advisers urged him not to refuse Attlee's hypothetical request. In the event, the government staggered through eighteen months with its bare majority and the Conservatives showed themselves keener to discredit than to defeat it. For a while, Attlee retained a great part of his esteem and authority but the unpopular economies contingent on the Korean war completed the public disenchantment.

In 1952, R.H. Tawney, a life-long Labour supporter, could look back and claim 1945–51 as the culmination of British Socialism. Although, on a longer view, he exaggerated, the transition to a planned economy and a welfare state was substantial. The government was clearly right to have done as much as it could in the first two years (contrary to the King's advice), because conditions after 1947 were never so favourable again. Its impetus, too, was destroyed by the external forces of the world economy rather than by weaknesses at home. But against that, it had failed to inspire a truly social change: educational opportunities and the distribution of wealth remained much as they had been at the end of the war. An integrated road-rail transport system did not emerge; despite the export drive, the dollar gap was not bridged. Worst, from the point of view of the electorate, the standard of life had not been maintained at a level regarded by 1951 as tolerable, certainly not in comparison with Western European countries.

As voters swung towards a Conservative Party bearing promises of a 'bonfire of controls' and an age of material prosperity, it could be seen that many of the old assumptions about politics and society had been strengthened after the fluid period of the mid 1940s when almost any change had seemed possible. A government after the 1951 election which included the radical and outstanding Conservatives of the 1930s, Harold Macmillan, Anthony Eden and R. A. Butler, forecast the continuing importance attached to Britain's great power status, combined at the same time with acceptance of most of the Labour Party's work in the fields of welfare and economic management. The future of the British monarchy in such circumstances was secure.

7 Terms for Survival
1945-51

GEORGE VI'S SUGGESTION that he understood the mood of the country as well as his Labour Prime Minister was open to debate but there could be no doubt that he had earned the right to have his advice on foreign affairs listened to with respect. By 1950 his experience stretched back more than thirty years, if his awareness during his father's reign is taken into account; and continuity of contact with Foreign Office papers proved a great advantage when compared with the briefer span of most ministers' experience. Lord Halifax, who always reported direct to the King on his return from Washington, as a friendly act as well as a duty, once wrote: 'Few people were endowed with judgment more wise or penetrating than his, rooted in simple and assured standards and frequently salted with humour, uninhibited and robust.'

The old dynastic ties which Queen Victoria had exploited, and through which Edward VII had been of value to British government interests, no longer signified and George VI could exercise influence in foreign – as distinct from Commonwealth – affairs only in so far as his advice made sense in the context of the post-war British predicament. He was fortunate, therefore, in the appointment of Ernest Bevin as Foreign Secretary, because Bevin shared his three great preoccupations: mistrust of Soviet Russia and awareness of the needs to rebuild Europe and maintain a close *entente* with the United States.

The King's determination that Britain's role in the world should not be diminished, in spite of the lessened influence evident at Yalta, showed during the Potsdam Conference. Keen to restore with Truman the accord he had had with Roosevelt, the King invited the President to a meeting before the conference opened. Russian suspicions of 'ganging up' between the Western Allies, however, prevented this, and the King's alternative suggestion, that he should review his troops in Germany and meet Stalin and Truman together, was vetoed because Montgomery could not answer for his safety in devastated Berlin. The meeting had to wait until, in the end, it took the form of a luncheon on board HMS *Renown* at Plymouth, significantly the only moment which Truman could spare as he hastened home for the dropping of the atomic bombs on Japan – a decision in which Britain, though a partner in atomic development, was consulted only as a formality.

PREVIOUS PAGES British troops move up towards the front to relieve American units in the Korean War.

OPPOSITE The King and President Truman aboard HMS *Renown* in Plymouth Sound, where the President stopped on his way home from the Potsdam Conference.

Potsdam revealed that inter-allied co-operation had evaporated. Russia intended to hold on to her gains in Eastern Europe. Britain was forced to concede to the reality of force her original war aims; and to recognise as legitimate the Soviet-dominated Lublin Government in Poland. The consequences of Yalta and the implicit recognition of separate spheres of influence could now be seen as the Allies resolved themselves into two hostile camps, confronting each other down the middle of Germany. But for two years after the end of the war, the United States showed a reluctance to accept the role of supporter of either British or European defence.

The experience of 1918, when Britain and France had been able to dominate the Paris Peace Conference after the withdrawal of President Wilson, could not be repeated. A war-torn, economically shattered Europe could not, over-night, be re-built as a counterweight to Russian territorial ambitions. Nor could Britain sustain such an effort: her client relationship with the United States in financial matters virtually precluded the spending of sufficient sums on rearmament or aid, even if these had been politically acceptable at home. Britain's own commitments elsewhere, in the Middle and Far East, Africa and the rest of the Commonwealth, far exceeded her real resources. Her armed forces overseas proved a constant drain on foreign currency reserves and manpower, both of which were desperately needed for economic recovery; yet it was as impossible simply to withdraw from the trouble centres of Palestine or India as it was to think of abandoning the defence of the British sector of West Germany. These were the obligations of a world power with a seat at the top table. Thus the often conflicting aims of post-war policy were defined: co-operation with Russia where (and if) it was possible; pressure on the United States to assume more of the burden; support for the United Nations and for schemes of European recovery.

At first Bevin had hopes of an accommodation with Russia. Not for nothing had he told the Labour Party Conference in 1945 'Left understands Left.' But the pre-war need for sympathetic allies which had brought Russia into the League of Nations in 1934 had vanished. The hope that, despite mutual conflicts, a cautious relationship with Britain like that between employers and trades unionists could be worked out, foundered on great clashes of interest in the Middle East and in Germany. In 1946 Bevin failed to get the Anglo-Soviet Treaty extended; the subsequent line-up of France and Britain over the terms of Marshall Aid went far to ensure that Russia and the satellite countries rejected it. Most seriously, the two sides struggled over the disposition of Germany, since both feared to lose the heartland of Europe to an alien ideology. The rift was confirmed by the deliberate creation of two separate political and economic entities, East and West Germany, and by the long trial of strength over Berlin in which the air lift, in 1948–9, saved the interests of the Western allies.

By that time, the United States had been committed to European defence as well as to recovery under the Marshall Aid programme. Initially, the American government had responded coldly, following Roosevelt's attitude at Yalta, to hints of the need for an Anglo-British front against Russia. Churchill's famous speech at Fulton, Missouri in March 1946, which proclaimed the existence of the Iron Curtain and Russia's aggressive intentions, was not at first taken seriously in the USA. Many Americans preferred to believe in a plot to entice their country's wealth in support of British imperialism, as the Anglo-Russian confrontation developed from the Balkans to the Persian Gulf. The endless wranglings over a peace settlement in the Middle East offered evidence in support of this thesis, because British interests seemed to attract the most virulent Soviet propaganda.

Refugee Arab camps in Transjordan, June 1949. The Arab antagonism to the new state of Israel was one of the factors leading to British withdrawal.

Above all, the American public was not interested: a Gallup Poll in October 1945 showed that only seven per cent rated foreign issues as more important than domestic, compared with forty-seven per cent in December 1939.

There is only limited truth in the view that Bevin's diplomacy and British strength held the ring for two years until the United States was weaned away from isolationism in 1947. Marshall Aid owed its timing more to recognition of long-term American economic interests; the partition of Germany and the Soviet take-over in Czechoslovakia were the material factors behind American support of the Brussels Treaty and the security arrangements elaborated within the United Nations Charter for the defence of free nations, which culminated in August 1949 in the North Atlantic Pact. This is not to say that Britain had no influence at all on American policy, rather that existing influence was not renewable. The defence of Greece and Turkey provides a good example. In 1947, the Labour Cabinet, beset by economic crises, looked overseas to liquidate what commitments it could. Palestine offered one example where there seemed no alternative but to withdraw in the face of intolerable difficulties. The cessation of aid to Greece and Turkey offered further possible economies, but the Cabinet feared that both countries would fall into the Soviet orbit if the United States did not fill the gap. With a certain self-righteousness (Dalton argued that Britain was propping up both Germany and south-eastern Europe, spending at interest American loan money which the United States ought to have been spending herself), the Americans were informed. The US government unwillingly obliged. Truman expressed his well-known doctrine of the defence of free institutions and a free way of life against Communism and backed it up by a virtually open-ended commitment on the part of the United States. But the Truman doctrine did not extend to the Middle East. Britain had to face up to the depredations of Arab and Iranian nationalism and the seizure of her oil installations at Abadan in 1951. Her power rested on the tenuous and ill-defined base of oil, the Suez Canal and the Baghdad Pact until it was finally liquidated in the aftermath of the Suez affair in 1956.

Governed by such constraints, British statesmen could only aspire to control events, although their public views claimed

far more freedom of action than actually existed. Bevin indeed never descended to the specious arguments about 'moral leadership of the world' and 'holding the balance between East and West', last resort of governments of the fifties and early sixties. But Bevin died, worn out by his struggles, in 1951, soon after the outbreak of the Korean war. It was an ineluctable fact of life that Britain could not for long depend economically on the United States and retain the style and weight of third greatest power, over and above other industrial nations. The true position was shown by the inability to aid either Greece or Turkey after 1947 and by the patent absurdity of borrowing in order to maintain the military presence in Germany which helped to give Britain her status: hence the importance of links with Europe, the 1947 defence treaty with France and the beginnings of economic co-operation. But Britain's approach to European unity was cursed with a fatal ambiguity. Although Bevin declared in January 1948: 'Great Britain cannot stand outside Europe and regard her problems as quite separate from those of her European neighbours', the actual commitment to the Brussels Treaty in March 1948 stopped short of anything smacking of political integration. Even the United European Movement, powerfully supported by Churchill, was more a vehicle of Conservative opposition to Labour than a genuine commitment to European integration. The Labour Government believed firmly that Britain had separate interests in the outside world and the Commonwealth, which European nations did not share, and a distinctive 'special relationship' with the United States. The fact that these assumptions were in conflict with the American Government's own preferences for European integration was only another symptom of how hard it was for post-war politicians to assess the true position.

In all these vicissitudes, the King remained firmly representative of Britain's great power status. His feelings about Russia never changed. He thoroughly approved what Churchill had done: 'We talked about his American visit and his Fulton speech', the King wrote in March 1946. 'I was able to tell him how much good it had done in the world and that Stalin's tirade against him personally, showed he had a guilty conscience.' Preparations for European defence preoccupied him until his death and he frequently criticised the French for evading what he believed were their responsibilities. He derived satisfaction from the fact that by 1949 even the left wing of the Labour Party had acknowledged the existence of the Cold War. The great revolution in American foreign policy, and the abandonment of isolation, seemed heaven-sent even if the corollary was that Britain must undergo the experience of becoming a second-rank power.

This did not mean that he approved automatically of the direction of American policy. The King gave full support to Attlee in his unquestioning response to the Communist invasion of South Korea in June 1950: 'It is naked aggression and it must be checked', Attlee told the House of Commons. But whereas the government followed the United Nations' mandate for the recovery of South Korea, to the tune of a defence budget of £3,400 million over three years, with grave consequences for economic recovery, the threat of a third world war, posed by the commitment of the Chinese army to stop General MacArthur's advance across the 38th Parallel into North Korean territory, brought about a reappraisal. Fearing the consequences of the all-out policy of the US military chiefs, Attlee flew to Washington. But the American government demanded compliance, not independence, and the limits of British power were shown all too clearly. Attlee met criticism of the paucity of the British war contribution, despite its successes, and found no support for admitting Communist China to the United Nations. The most he could gain was a vague undertaking from Truman not to use the atomic bomb.

Commonwealth events occupied a large part of George VI's concern in the six years after the war. The first majority Labour Government was expected to carry out the promises of independence and decolonialisation echoed in its pre-war manifestos. Fortunately, this stage in the shedding of the imperial mission brought few conflicts between them and the titular head of the Commonwealth. George VI was never an imperialist. His father had opposed the Morley-Minto reforms in India and had occupied an exalted, almost hieratic position as King-Emperor; but however much George VI had been influenced by the ideas of Lord Milner or Joseph Chamberlain, he recognised by the 1930s that the future of the Empire could

179

lie only in Commonwealth associations. For the Colonies, on the other hand, particularly in East Africa, he envisaged continued British control. Few imagined that the 'wind of change' was only twelve years away, following on the independence of Ghana in 1957. Even predominantly white Southern Rhodesia did not seem likely to be able to count on Dominion status for a generation.

Dominions' participation in the war in no way altered the trend of each of them towards distinctive aims and policies. Defence strategy still provided a high-level bridge with Britain, but otherwise the principal value of the connexion, from the Dominions' point of view, lay in the economic interchange of trading preferences dating from 1932 and, more particularly for third world countries within the sterling area, in access to a source of development capital. For all members, especially the smaller units, the Commonwealth provided a sounding board for grievances and a framework in which collective power could be exercised. The British derived from it a sense of mission: of responsibility towards, and power from, an aggregation of countries which had nothing to do with the growing political and ideological divisions of the rest of the world.

These calculations rested, rather more soundly than in the 1930s, on a mutual balance of advantage as well as on less definable links of tradition and sentiment. But the post-war balance was not achieved without disharmonies. Britain's rout in the Far East in 1941–2 brought about an irrevocable loss of prestige. Rule in commercially vital Singapore, Malaya and Hong Kong could be restored but elsewhere the effort was pointless. Burma left the Commonwealth altogether in 1947 and the British fortunately avoided the French error of trying, by the war in Indo-China, to recover what had been lost. Ireland went too, with the repeal of 'external association' in 1948; but in practice, for all the heat of the trade war of the thirties, this had been a consequence of 1921. In contrast, the futures of Australia, South Africa and India posed problems capable of solution.

Australia asserted her independence during the war when John Curtin, Prime Minister from 1941–5, demanded a seat on the British War Cabinet, claiming that his country was being   OPPOSITE King George VI.

181

denied proper defence against the Japanese. Churchill refused. Curtin's threat to seek a defence agreement with the United States gave the King a great deal of worry, but it was answered for a time by the creation of a Pacific War Council. Nevertheless, Australia and New Zealand were included inevitably in the American Pacific line-up against Chinese encroachment in South-East Asia, by the Anzus Pact of 1951 and the American-sponsored South-East Asia Treaty Organisation Pact, signed at Manila in April 1954. If anything, American anti-Communism helped to preserve the links between these Dominions and Britain – but only so long as Britain acknowledged identity with American aims.

The threat of the South African Nationalist Party, led by Dr Malan, to secede altogether from the Commonwealth after the war, could be contained only by the slender margin of Smuts's Parliamentary majority. The experiment in conciliation begun in 1909 by the Peace of Vereeniging could be seen to have failed, as the Nationalists emerged from the economic nightmare of the Boer farmers of the thirties, and the political restrictions of the war, quite unreconciled to English-speaking domination. Once more therefore, as in Canada in 1939, the royal touch was tried. Smuts had often discussed with the King a visit to open the South African Parliament, and the Governor General, Gideon Van Zyl, sent a formal invitation for the spring of 1947.

This news polarised opinion. As the preparations began for receiving the King, the Queen and the two Princesses, the Nationalist Press complained bitterly of a blatant manœuvre to strengthen monarchic feeling. Afrikaner leaders announced that they would boycott the ceremony. How much store the King set by the visit may be judged from the fact that he left Britain in a critical year and risked the accusation that the royal family was basking in South African sunshine during that terrible winter. (He did, in fact, suggest returning early but Attlee advised against, fearing that the publicity would make even more of a crisis out of the fuel shortage.)

The royal party sailed to South Africa in the newly-commissioned battleship *Vanguard*. From the outset, when the King decorated Smuts with the Order of Merit, the Nationalists were marked by their absence and the King responded by making every personal effort he could at reconciliation. In

Groote Schuur, Cecil Rhodes's magnificent house at the foot
of Table Mountain, he presented Smuts with President
Kruger's Bible, captured by the British during the Boer War,
and, in a gesture entirely his own, he paid a courteous visit to
the aged widow of Martinus Steyn, last President of the independent Orange Free State. Slowly, a little warmth was
generated. By the end, he had encountered some personal
cordiality, though little on an official level. The tour, which
extended far beyond South Africa, was otherwise an enthusiastic success. The King climbed Table Mountain, visited
Mont aux Sources Park in the Drakensberg Mountains, with
the indefatigable old Field Marshal, opened the Southern
Rhodesian Parliament in Salisbury, visited the Victoria Falls
and passed through a hundred native villages from Zululand
in the east to Basutoland on the edge of the Kalahari Desert.
Appropriately, the journey ended with Princess Elizabeth's
coming-of-age ceremony, held in Cape Town, during which
she broadcast, *urbe et orbe*, to South Africa and the Commonwealth, a simple and moving statement of dedication to her
future duty.

Field Marshal Smuts leads the King and Queen to the top of Table Mountain. The Cape of Good Hope is in the background.

While it could in no way prevent, the royal visit may have helped to diminish, the Nationalist victory at the 1948 election and may have done something to retain South Africa within the Commonwealth, at least as long as other members could stomach the Nationalists' policy of *apartheid*, which unrolled in swingeing legislation during the 1950s. The King's personal popularity at least was firmly established. During his last illness, Dr Malan invited him back to South Africa to recuperate as a guest of the government, and a visit was arranged for 1951.

The biggest question in the King's lifetime concerned the future of India. The 1935 Act had not been implemented before the war, partly because the more self-seeking princes refused to participate and partly because the Congress Party, led by Nehru and Gandhi, was unable to take overall responsibility. The Muslim League, fearful of being subjected to the Hindu majority, began its long search for a separate territory through partition. A decade of hatred and violence had already made an understanding between them almost impossible and co-operation reached such an ebb that in September 1939 the Viceroy had to declare war against Germany on his own author-

ity. The Congress leaders at once withdrew. Subsequent events cast doubts on whether India could even be held during the war, because while the Muslims openly demanded partition, the Congress Party put strong pressure on Britain's allies, Nationalist China and the United States. In 1942 Churchill was forced to promise Dominion status for the end of the war.

Zulu warriors greet the King at Eshowe, capital of Zululand.

The King worried deeply about the implications of Hindu rule for the Muslim minority (who provided the greater part of the Indian army), the prospect of secession of the 'brightest jewel in the imperial crown', and the attitude of the princely states.

Many Indians [he wrote after a gloomy talk with Churchill] still want to owe allegiance to me as King Emperor. Winston is not satisfied with it, and told me he is not going to ask my approval for anything that will not help now and work later. It is a very important though difficult matter, and whatever is said now cannot please everybody and will have a bad repercussion on the Indian army, in Afghanistan, the North West Frontier and Nepal [that is, along the frontier with Soviet Russia]. Anything to upset the loyalty of the Gurkhas would be tragic.

185

The preliminary discussions undertaken before the declaration proved abortive. In spite of his obviously pro-Congress sympathies, the leader of the British mission, Sir Stafford Cripps, was unable to get agreement from the parties and the princes. The King was annoyed that Cripps had virtually ignored the Viceroy, but he accepted the value of the offer at that stage of the war. 'It has cleared up many ambiguities for the rest of the world, especially America, as to our rule in India', the King wrote tersely, 'The Hindus will now have to make up their minds whether to hinder our war effort or not.'

American support for Congress leaders lessened after their rejection of the Dominion status offer. But Congress now demanded total British withdrawal, and in Subhas Chandra Bose, pro-Japanese elements found a leader. The government was forced to intern both Gandhi and Nehru and to suppress with substantial bloodshed a series of revolts in the provinces, in order to hold India as a base for the Burma campaign against Japan. Military rule could be only a temporary expedient, as the King recognised when advising against Churchill's recommendation of Eden as the new Viceroy in 1943: he doubted 'if the political situation in India will yield to treatment at the hands of any individual statesman'. But George VI believed in firm rule so long as that rule lasted. He was fierce with Field Marshal Wavell (who was finally chosen as Viceroy) for proposing clemency and releasing the Congress leaders. He would not accept that India needed to be handed over pre-cipitately and he reproached Churchill, the once dedicated defender of British rule, with the words: 'I have always said India has got to be *governed* and that will have to be our policy.' Churchill, who understood better the implications of the revolts in 1942, discouraged him gently from proposing a visit to India towards the end of the war.

Later, the King recognised the inevitable. Yet at the end of the war, British disengagement seemed as impossible as con-tinued rule. The Labour Party was pledged to independence, but a conference at Simla in June 1945 achieved nothing, and elections only reinforced communal discords. The façade of interim government concealed reservations on both sides and when the King received Muslim and Hindu leaders at Bucking-ham Palace in December 1945, he began to envisage civil war.

OPPOSITE The royal party acknowledge the cheers from HMS *Vanguard* as they step ashore at Portsmouth after the South African tour.

186

He concluded, however, not that India was claiming too much, but that 'we have gone too fast for them'. Given that United India was still desirable, he may have been right. But the only alternative to partition – a solution still far from the minds of the British Cabinet – was military repression, irreconcilable with the aspirations of a Labour Government. So it was decided to withdraw with as little bloodshed as possible. After a meeting with Attlee, the King minuted: 'The Indian leaders have got to learn that the responsibility is theirs and that they must learn how to govern.' Since this was only ten years after the anguished debates in Britain over the relatively mild extension of responsibility contained in the Government of India Act, the demands on Indian leaders seemed unreasonably high. But the war and the Indian political parties had left Britain no choice.

Unable to extract from the Labour Government a decision on the means, Wavell asked if he could set a firm date of March 1948 and gradually withdraw from the perimeter to Karachi and Bombay. The plan looked too much like a military retreat for Attlee who, concluding that Wavell was finished, sacked him and turned to Lord Mountbatten, the supreme commander in South-East Asia. Mountbatten was the King's cousin and his closest friend. He had hoped to become First Sea Lord like his father, Prince Louis of Battenberg, but under the King's enthusiastic persuasion, he agreed to take up the unenviable job of Viceroy. He asked for a free hand from the government to wind up the Raj, so long as it could be done peacefully.

The King was thus intimately involved in the final act, when the time-scale of transfer was shortened, to prevent civil war, and when partition became an unpleasant but necessary solution. With enormous energy and persuasive ability, Mountbatten induced Nehru and Jinnah, the Muslim leader, to agree. The final transfer of power took place on 15 August 1947. Even so, hundreds of thousands died in the ensuing slaughter, and millions became exiled refugees. This terrible vindication was palliated only by the realisation that Mountbatten's mission probably prevented worse.

Some consolation for the British, however, was provided by the wishes of both India and Pakistan to remain within the Commonwealth. Mountbatten's own part was recognised when Nehru invited him to stay on as India's first Governor

188

ABOVE Viscount Mount-
batten, the last Viceroy of
India, speaking to the
Constituent Assembly in
New Delhi.

RIGHT Jawarlal Nehru, the
first premier of India,
arriving at the Council
House Library, New Delhi.

General and he presided with skill and dignity over the first year of independence. Meanwhile, the King's title had to be altered, for he was no longer Emperor of India; to Attlee's surprise, he made not the slightest objection – 'A remarkable fact. It shows the great advantage of having a King who was never static but who moved with the times.'

A means had still to be found in the late 1940s to accommodate the republican constitutions of India, Pakistan and Ceylon. How were they to take action like the older Dominions, but not in the King's name, and how could they belong to an entity of which the King was head, if they could not recognise him as their ultimate sovereign? Some of the administrative problems were met by the formation of the Commonwealth Relations Office but for a time there was a real danger that India, for whom a neutralist foreign policy was peculiarly important,

The Commonwealth prime ministers in the State Dining Room of Buckingham Palace, 1951. From left to right: Theophilus Donges for South Africa; Don Stephen Senanyake of Ceylon; Sir Godfrey Huggins of Southern Rhodesia; Sydney Holland of New Zealand; Robert Menzies of Australia; The Queen; The King; The Duchess of Kent; Louis St Laurent of Canada; Clement Attlee; Princess Margaret and Nehru of India.

might have to secede altogether. The King was adamant that she should be retained; yet the means had to be acceptable to all the other members of the Commonwealth. Goodwill was also essential, because Nehru made it clear that India was not prepared, like Ireland in 1921, to haggle over details: association must be on Indian terms or none. So the meeting between the King and Nehru which took place in October 1948 had more than ceremonial significance. If India went out of the Commonwealth, Russian influence might replace British, and SEATO defence would be devalued, to say nothing of the impact in Malaya. If India remained, by virtue of her size she would become a leader of a neutral grouping of immense political significance as a bridge in the Cold War. The warmth of the invitation which the King held out to Nehru was only one among many factors, and the haggling over terms lasted until the Commonwealth Prime Ministers' Conference in April 1949, when Attlee was able to bring Nehru into the persuasive contact of his future associates. But a formula was found. The King was to be head of the Commonwealth, not of India, and in that capacity, Indians would owe him allegiance. In the white drawing-room of Buckingham Palace on 26 April, the King was able to receive and commend the Prime Ministers' collective decision.

The Empire survived, transmuted into a multi-racial Commonwealth. Less coherent an assembly than it had been when George VI came to the throne, the Prime Ministers' Conference became perhaps a more important meeting-place, in which Britain took, year by year, a less dominant place. As head of the Commonwealth, the King had played no small part in the change.

OPPOSITE The King's coffin lies in state in Westminster Hall, February 1952.

8
The King in
his Country
1945-51

At the beginning of 1951, as Londoners planned for the Festival of Britain on the south bank of the Thames, it was possible to believe that the years of austerity were at last over. Clothes rationing had ended two years before, on the extravagant note of the New Look, and most of the remaining restrictions and rationing had been eased during 1950. A whole generation was growing up for whom everything from bananas to television sets was excitingly new, while those who remembered the elegance and comfort of pre-war middle- and upper-class life slowly turned from complaints that the old days had gone for good to other grumbles, about the price of the new ball-point pens (34/6) or the long delays on car deliveries caused by the Korean war.

The royal family had been most conscientious in conforming to the restrictions during the decade since 1940. They had always tried to share privations and danger in the war and in the peace it was known that, except for state occasions, petrol was husbanded carefully by the Household and that unappetising substitutes like whale meat also appeared on the Palace menu. The King was particularly sensitive at the thought that he was absent in South Africa during the 1946–7 winter. But austerity did not preclude gaiety. Princess Elizabeth and Princess Margaret took their part in private as well as state occasions and the royal family slowly restored the pre-war pattern, though not quite the former style of their entertainments. In June 1949, 'Chips' Channon attended a party of the Princesses' friends at the Palace:

> The rooms were banked with flowers and the lit vitrines full of china. Windows were open onto the terrace, and the cool air was a relief. ... We saw the King and Queen waiting to receive us, side by side: he seemed brown and she looked magnificent in a white satin semi-crinoline number with the Garter and splendid rubies.... We walked along a long passage, hung with Canalettos and Zoffanys by the dozen, many of which had been re-hung and cleaned since the war. The Chapel, Throne-room and Waterloo Chamber were all brightly lit ... the King had his foot up on a footstool to rest [after his operation], though he seemed quite well and often danced. The Queen danced every dance vigorously, but not as violently as Lady Astor who despite her seventy years seemed positively frivolous.

PREVIOUS PAGES The King and his family walk through the barley at Sandringham.

OPPOSITE King George riding with his daughters in Windsor Great Park in 1939.

196

The King with the Princesses
at the Royal Lodge soon
after the war.

In the summer of 1950 he recorded: 'Ascot this year was highly enjoyable, and obviously the King, who now dotes on society and parties, adored it. He looked much younger than the Duke of Windsor.' The King was fifty-four then, apparently in the mid-term of his life. He had never seemed gayer or more elegant and his family life had been continually and happily fulfilled. This was so in public also: with some of George v's gruff pleasure at the unexpected warmth of the crowds during the jubilee ceremonies of 1935, the King confessed to amazement and pride at the reception of the Silver Wedding festivities in April 1948. A torrent of letters reached the Palace, expressing their authors' gratitude at what the royal family had meant to them during the grim past decade.

The King and Queen derived great pleasure from their children, with whom there were none of the awkward constraints of the King's own upbringing. During the war, cut off from the Princesses at Windsor, the King and Queen had worried that they might miss a vital part of their youth, but they took what chances there were of reunion. The King went as often as he could to their parties, rode with them in Windsor Great Park and reaped the benefit after the war ended, in their companionship as grown-ups. He was the best of fathers, who treated his children with respect, love and firmness, to whom his children talked as an equal. He could be firm, even stern, yet he allowed his daughters far greater freedom than he himself had known, and he encouraged them to use it well. His only unvarying requirement was that they should show a dedication to the public side of life equal to his own.

Princess Elizabeth never became Princess of Wales – that, as the King said, was the title due to the Prince of Wales's wife – but she was heir presumptive to the throne and her marriage could not be anything but a matter of keen concern to the King. She first met Prince Philip, a cousin of the King of Greece, whose mother was Lord Mountbatten's sister, in 1939 and by 1945 it was no secret in the family that they wished to marry. Judging them both to be too young, the King preferred for them to wait. There were certain difficulties about Prince Philip's status, which had also to be resolved. He had been born in 1921 in Corfu, then exiled in Paris, and from the age of eight brought up within the Mountbatten family. Because of his Greek

A family group at the wedding of Princess Elizabeth and Prince Philip, Duke of Edinburgh. Princess Margaret is the chief bridesmaid. The King and Queen and the Duke of Gloucester are to the right of Prince Philip while Queen Mary stands behind the bride. Prince Philip's uncle, Lord Mountbatten, stands at the left edge of the curtain.

birth, his distinguished career with the navy had been possible only under war-time regulations and he wished to become a British subject, with a permanent commission. The uneasy situation in Greece, after British intervention against the Communists in 1944, made naturalisation politically difficult until 1947. Then at his own request he was known simply as Lieutenant Philip Mountbatten.

Even then, the King hesitated before giving his consent, unwilling for his older daughter to marry the first man she had met. Their determination was so great, however, that after the South African tour their engagement was announced and the wedding date set for November 1947. The King, who took a lively interest in the orders of chivalry, presented Princess Elizabeth with the Order of the Garter before the wedding in the Abbey; and granted Lieutenant Philip the title of His Royal Highness the Duke of Edinburgh. Once more the crowned heads of Europe came to London, fewer in number than before the war and many from exile, but no less resplendent, and the pageantry in the streets did something to brighten the winter of that otherwise dismal year.

During their honeymoon, the King wrote a touching valediction: 'Your leaving us has left a great blank in our lives but do remember that your old house is still yours and do come back to it as much and as often as possible. I can see that you are sublimely happy with Philip, which is right, but don't forget us, is the wish of your everloving and devoted papa.' This wish was amply fulfilled and in 1948, after the birth of Princess Elizabeth's first child, Prince Charles, he was able to dote on his grandchild as Edward VII had on him.

With foresight, and in the most natural way, George VI prepared Princess Elizabeth for her future duties. During his successive illnesses, she was able to stand in for him and she took her first salute at the Trooping of the Colour in June 1949. With the Duke of Edinburgh she toured Canada in 1951, and when the King's operation forced him to cancel the royal tour of Australia and New Zealand, which had been arranged for the following year, she was able to set off on – though not to complete – the journey in his place. Although the King had no knowledge of how ill he was, he arranged for both the Princess

Prince Charles and Princess Anne with their grandparents in November 1951, the first picture taken after the King's operation.

and the Duke to be introduced as Privy Councillors, and it was fitting that she should have had her first brief experience of state affairs under her father's guidance.

Looking back from the late 1940s, it could be seen that George VI had grown steadily into the practice of kingship and become, in a little over ten years, the standard by which the monarchy itself was to be measured. He was careful, even jealous of the rights and privileges which he had inherited, and regarded it as a prime duty to pass them on unimpaired. Like his father, he treated critically anything which appeared derogatory or sloppy in the respect due to his status. Equally he was precise and careful in his attention to the constitutional proprieties. The details of ceremony or dress attracted particular attention: any oversight in the order of precedence, or of medal ribbons, or the way an officer wore his sword on parade, caused a rebuke whose gentle smile did not disguise displeasure. He could spot the wrongly-pressed pleats of a piper's kilt at the Ghillies' Ball at Balmoral as soon as he came into the room. His own suits were always beautifully cut and worn with elegance and style. Although not a leader of fashion like Edward VII, he took a lively interest in design, and detailed the wartime livery for the royal household.

In appearance as in character, George VI matured with age. To the end of his life he retained a lithe, slim figure and his fine features show particularly well in photographs. Whether on a horse, walking or relaxed in a chair, he gave the impression of controlled energy and finesse. His concern with the proper ordering of things extended to orders and decorations. The designing of the George Cross, like the Stalingrad Sword, gave him particular pleasure. He had always wanted to detach the the Garter, highest order of all, from the political connotation which it had acquired as part of the patronage at the disposal of the Prime Minister, and to restore it as a specifically Christian and royal gift. (In the past, Edward VII had, under some protest, followed his ministers' advice and bestowed it on the Shah of Persia.) The advent of a Labour Government, chary of the award of honours, gave him the chance and by agreement with the party leaders, not only the Garter but the Thistle and the Patrick reverted to the same footing as the Order of Merit. The King also restored the practice of regular gatherings of the

Order and oversaw the splendid ceremonies of the six hundredth anniversary in 1948.

On the evidence of his diary, George VI was a more human and pungent commentator on paper than his father, but he rarely allowed his feelings about the public side of his life to escape. Except when he wished to give advice, stating his reasons, he refrained from comment. In an age which set greater store by discretion than the generation before 1914, and in which the functions of monarchy became more stylised in proportion to their diminished political importance, the King's private secretaries showed themselves more discreet than their predecessors – than, for example, Sir Arthur Ponsonby, whose memoirs give a penetrating view of the characters of Queen Victoria and Edward VII. Thus it is not easy to penetrate the dignified, official picture constructed by contemporary adulation and the respectful official biography. It is clear that the King's judgment improved both in public affairs and in such private tastes as artistic appreciation. Few British sovereigns have been great collectors since the days of Charles I, and George VI's tastes remained traditional. But after the war, he busied himself with the restoration of the long neglected royal collection of pictures. He used often to watch the restorers at work on certain favourite paintings and he decided on their positioning, even going back to the archives to find where the Gainsboroughs or Hoppners had originally been hung.

George VI was genuinely and deeply religious. From his youth he had also been a Freemason, sometime Grand Master of Middlesex province, continuing a royal tradition begun in 1782 by the Duke of Cumberland. The symbolism and morality of Freemasonry blended easily with his own religious practice. Like George V, he was a regular attender at church and he demanded the same standards from others. Perhaps because of this, to many people in the 1950s, the royal family was beginning to appear a little old fashioned. Yet this was an unfair judgment because the King was by no means averse to ecumenical association. He regarded Cardinal Hinsley, Archbishop of Westminster, with great respect and was most upset when old Protestant traditions were (successfully) argued against his sending a representative to the Requiem Mass held for the Cardinal in 1943.

The lighter side of the King's life fitted well with the gradual emancipation of British manners after the war. His sense of fun was discreet – he had long outgrown the practical joking in which Edward VII indulged all his life; equally, he lacked his father's enjoyment of ribaldry which caused him, literally, to burst a stitch after his operation in 1929, at one of the stories told by the Lord Privy Seal, J.H. Thomas. No one has recorded a *bon mot* as good as George V's comment on the Hoare-Laval débâcle in 1935: 'No more coals to Newcastle, no more Hoares to Paris.' But George VI's conversation was forthright and entertaining: he possessed the priceless gift of being interested in whoever he was talking to, and no one sitting next to him ever had to fear the chilling signs of royal boredom. He loved dancing and would often lead the conga at his daughters' parties. His taste in entertainment – in common with the vast majority of his people – embraced ITMA, Tommy Handley and the Crazy Gang, and the style of Royal Variety Shows long after his death followed the patterns he had enjoyed.

There was a whole side of the King's life rarely open to the public. Well before the war, Baldwin told Thomas Jones, 'The King is a family man and he hopes he may keep his Lodge at Windsor as a retreat from the public glare.' In the end, Sandringham and Balmoral became the real retreats, where he was able to become, during the sixteen years of his reign, not only a family man but a country land-owner. He lacked the gift for hobbies. Whereas his father had created one of the finest stamp collections in the world and his grandfather had pursued success on the turf as far as winning the Derby, George VI enjoyed both stamps and racing without very great enthusiasm. Instead, all that energy went into the development and management of the royal estates, especially in Norfolk. With meticulous care, he kept pace with the details of farming, tenancies and improvements of estate cottages. Very little was done, at either Sandringham or Balmoral, of which he was not aware. Among the factors in Scotland, or the managers and tenant farmers in the south, he was able 'to put off the King'. It could be said of him that, like Charles II, 'He might be seen of a morning before lunch, with a great crowd of his people about him, and here he would listen to all comers.' The interest in landscape gardening increased steadily after the first tentative essays at Royal

OPPOSITE The King's favourite entertainers were Tommy Handley (above), with the cast of ITMA), and the Crazy Gang (below).

Lodge in the 1920s, and such links ensured the friendship of men like the great land-owner and Foreign Secretary Edward Halifax, a friendship rooted in a common love and understanding of the countryside. When the King died, Lord Halifax erected a memorial to him, as an act of personal piety, on a hill on his Garrowby estate in Yorkshire.

Shooting was the King's favourite sport. Brought up in the rigid 1900s when fat, low, homebred pheasants, driven in great assemblies over the guns of Sandringham delighted Edward VII, he gradually learned the ways of wild birds and created a very different shooting environment when, as King, he was able to reorder the Sandringham coverts and start from scratch with the grouse-moors at Balmoral. Stalking, as a young man, taught him the wildness and solitariness of the Scottish moors and he discerned the importance of wind and changing weather in rough shooting with the Queen's family at Glamis. He was always an excellent shot, very quick onto the bird, and he never shirked experiment or long days walking for a mixed bag. His passion for organisation found full expression in the holidays at Balmoral where he would plan the day's sport and the whole scenario of ponies, lunch and beaters for the drive. He taught Prince Philip to shoot and it is a sound commentary on his skill that the meticulous royal game books show that he shot over a thousand woodcock, most wary and difficult of birds, in his lifetime. He delighted especially in wild-fowling in Norfolk and the comments below the record of the day show that he was not a fair-weather shot. An entry for December 1938 is typical: 'Snow and a very cold east wind. I spent four hours in a hide in a kale field.'

The King did what he could to abolish the outdated habit of competition between one gun and another. On his own estates and as a guest elsewhere, he helped to achieve the transition from the Edwardian fashion for amassing great heaps of slaughtered easy pheasants to the rough shooting and mixed days of the last twenty years. And he became, like most fine shots since the days of the great Captain Peter Hawker in the nineteenth century, something of a naturalist. A friend who was a constant guest at Balmoral wrote: 'He derived, I think, infinite satisfaction (as most people do) from the performance of what he did well, and this zest found him always equally eager, whether he had drawn

OPPOSITE The King surveys his farm stock. He took a detailed interest in the management of the royal estates, particularly at Sandringham and Balmoral.

The Royal Festival Hall was the only permanent building among the many erected for the Festival of Britain on the South Bank site.

the best place in a good partridge drive, or was shooting a few rabbits at Sandringham, when pheasant shooting was finished.'

The Festival of Britain was dedicated by the King and Queen at a service in St Paul's Cathedral on 3 May 1951, exactly a century after the Great Exhibition of 1851. The organisers had wanted the King to perform the ceremony on Tower Hill and sail up river in the state barge but he replied forthrightly that Tower Hill had too many bloody associations and that anyway the state barge leaked. The time seemed unpropitious for celebration: the Labour Government was writhing like an old wounded animal gnawing at its injuries; Ernest Bevin had just died and Aneurin Bevan had resigned, splitting the government further; and the lists of the wounded and dead were still coming in from the terrible fighting in Korea along the Imjin river. The South Bank site itself was incomplete and as the crowds advanced after the private view, they did so through debris left by the retreating workmen. But the Festival, conceived by its architect and director general, Gerald Barry, as an antidote of 'fun, fantasy and colour' to the universal greyness of the previous decade, proved to be an astonishing success. The knocking campaign against the alleged extravagance of the South Bank and the Battersea pleasure gardens had been only partly answered in 1950 when the King and Queen became patrons; and at the last moment doubts, strikes and economies nearly brought the whole plan to a halt. But the lights and music across the river drew crowds as if the pleasure gardens had been Xanadu, and the piazzas, the Skylon and the Dome of Discovery showed that modern British architecture had at last grown out of neo-Georgian traditionalism.

For many commentators, the Festival marked the end of the hungry forties and the start of a new enlightened era. Festival symbolism spread everywhere in Britain in the summer of 1951 as over eight million people visited the South Bank site and the gardens. It *was* a turning point of sorts. As the organisers had seen from the beginning: 'One mistake we should *not* make, we should not fall into the error of supposing we are going to produce anything conclusive. In this sceptical age, the glorious assurance of the mid-Victorians would find no echo.' But the future did not belong to the liberal intellectuals who had conceived and designed the Festival any more than to the dying Labour administration which paid the bill. The gardens were torn down, and instead of the fondly-desired National Theatre, the site lay derelict for nine years, until it was submerged under one of the ugliest office blocks in Europe and a car park for seven hundred cars. The King, who had opened the Festival, was too ill to attend the final night in September when enormous crowds massed to hear the closing caberet sung by Gracie Fields – another voice from a rapidly vanishing past.

Gracie Fields, star of the war years and beyond.

The future, or at least the next thirteen years, was settled by a narrow margin at the General Election in October 1951. Worn out by the guerrilla tactics of the Conservative opposition, and wracked by squabbles, of which Bevan's resignation on the issue of National Health Service charges was the fiercest, the Labour Government had long lost its freedom of action. Worried that his tour of Australia and New Zealand might mean absence during a political crisis, the King twice asked Attlee whether he intended to ask for a dissolution. Attlee made up his mind during the summer recess, and the polling date was set for 21 October. (By then, the seriousness of the King's illness was known and the royal tour postponed; his private secretary took some pains, therefore, to assure Attlee that no improper pressure had been brought on him to dissolve.) The result was clear, though far from overwhelming: Conservatives, 321; Labour, 295; Liberals, 6; others, 3. Churchill had a majority twice that of the outgoing administration.

On Attlee, the King conferred the mark of his personal esteem, the Order of Merit; but he was too ill to receive individually the retiring or incoming ministers or even to discuss with Churchill more than the senior Cabinet appointments. That November, the King's Speech was read by the Lord Chancellor. But there was no reason for the public to suspect that he was likely to die: and he convalesced rapidly during the winter. Given the mood of stock-taking which surrounded the year 1951, Lord Halifax was probably typical of many when he contrasted 'the bleak inauguration of his reign' with its peak. 'How great a work, with the Queen's help, the King had accomplished in the re-establishment of the monarchy. It is not easy to overstate the effect of their influence and example.'

In making a distinction between sound analysis and adulation, one must discard much contemporary comment. The jokes made by royalty are always laughed at, just as the slightest evidence of the common touch is seized on and magnified. The 1950s were to witness a distinct change in attitudes towards royalty of the British Press, which had begun, perhaps, soon after the break-down of the 'gentleman's agreement' during the Abdication, and which touched a level of bathos after George VI's death with the serialisation of chit-chat by retired servants from the Household and the ineffable memoirs of 'Crawfie'.

In this, the mass-circulation papers simply followed their American and French counterparts, though mercifully not to the level of *France Dimanche*. During George VI's reign, dignity was preserved. He would have been outraged as well as upset at the thought that unofficial photographs could be sold for a small fortune on the Continent, and that the royal family would have no recourse against bad manners and worse taste. Yet this was in itself a symptom of his success in transmuting the institution of monarchy into its modern shape. The monarchy was news: and in the twenty years after George VI's death, the royal family had to learn to live with the implications of the public demand for news. George VI's distinction lay in the fact that he kept alive Bagehot's 'mystique of monarchy' in an era of popularisation, without having to adopt what he regarded as the excessively informal habits of the Scandinavian royal families. The questions opened up before the death of George V and left unanswered during the brief reign of Edward VIII were either settled or no longer relevant. The social level of the King's affiliations, the cost of monarchy and management of the royal estates, might cause occasional criticism or arouse a few Parliamentary questions, but were no longer likely, as Lord Esher had feared in 1918, to shake the monarchy's position. Equally, the greater risk that the monarchy might prove to be irrelevant had also disappeared. If the King could achieve a sound working relationship with a majority Labour Government, there could be little concern for the flexibility of the institution. Attlee's prosaic tribute after the King's death was worth many more flowery phrases: 'Few people realise how much time and care he gave to public affairs, but visitors from overseas were often astonished at his close familiarity with all kinds of questions. With this close study went a good judgment and a sure instinct for what was really vital.' If there had been a moment for a republic, it would have been 1945: but a situation in which that could have happened would have demanded a different King, with a different war record.

'Time has been' said the brazen head in the *Tale of Friar Bacon and Friar Bungay*. George VI underwent his first major operation for arterio-sclerosis in March 1949. He had never fully recovered from the strains of the war, and had lost over a stone

in weight during the South African tour. At first the doctors thought that his right leg might have to be amputated, but the operation, conducted by Professor James Learmouth, after some months of rest and treatment, was apparently successful. But although he recovered well and was able to shoot again, he knew that a second thrombosis might be fatal, and in Scotland he abandoned hill-walking for a pony or Landrover. More serious symptoms showed in the middle of 1951. In spite of compliance with Learmouth's instructions, the King lost weight again and grew increasingly tired and grey. He seemed to have lost the power of recuperation. 'The incessant worries and crises through which we have to live got me down properly', he wrote to a friend. He caught influenza, yet insisted on appearing at the installation of his brother, the Duke of Gloucester, as Great Master of the Order of the Bath, in Westminster Abbey at the end of May. Later, the doctors found inflammation in the left lung. That summer, even the bracing air of Balmoral failed to revive him fully. A doctors' conference early in September was followed by an urgent summons to London where Mr Price Thomas, the lung specialist, diagnosed cancer. The King probably never knew the nature of the disease but submitted to another operation for the removal of the left lung on 23 September. In spite of the ever-present danger of thrombosis, and the fact that some of the nerves in his larynx had to be severed, the King recovered and could soon speak almost normally. In October, he was able to congratulate his doctors and nurses on their solicitude and to look forward to a return to some public duties, with the prospect of the second half of the winter in South Africa. He spent a happy, carefree Christmas at Sandringham; but his Christmas broadcast had to be recorded piece by piece, to obviate undue strain on his voice. He was even allowed to shoot and, on the first visit to a theatre since his illness, to enjoy *South Pacific* at Drury Lane. Unable to resist saying goodbye to Princess Elizabeth and the Duke of Edinburgh on their journey to Australia, preceded by a short tour of East Africa, he stood at London Airport before returning to Sandringham, and the last photographs show him windswept and haggard in the January gale. On 5 February, a cold, crisp sunny day, he shot hares as well as he had ever done; and that night, quite peacefully, he died.

OPPOSITE The last pictures taken of the King were at London airport, where he waved goodbye to Princess Elizabeth and Prince Philip as they left for Kenya.

213

A Royal Funeral

In death as in life, ceremony surrounded the King. As tributes flowed in from all over the world florists were busy preparing the magnificent wreaths (below); the Scots Guards stood with reversed arms and bowed heads at Chelsea Barracks, rehearsing for the King's funeral (opposite); shopkeepers draped the royal arms in black (right). Meanwhile, at Sandringham the late King's tenants escorted his body to Wolferton station (opposite below).

ABOVE The funeral procession marches up to Marble Arch
on its way to Paddington Station for the journey to Windsor.

Out in Kenya, the government received a telegram, sent *en clair*: 'Flash Emergency. Mr Churchill with his humble duty offers to your Majesty the profound condolences of the Cabinet on the death of your dear father the King. The Accession Council will meet this afternoon at St James's Palace to proclaim your Majesty's accession. The Cabinet in all things awaits your Majesty's commands.'

RIGHT The new Queen, Elizabeth II.

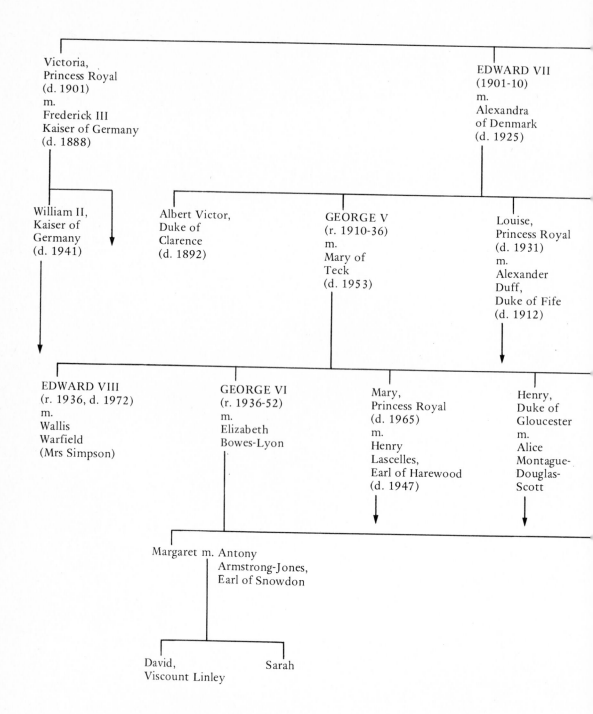

Victoria,
Princess Royal
(d. 1901)
m.
Frederick III
Kaiser of Germany
(d. 1888)

EDWARD VII
(1901-10)
m.
Alexandra
of Denmark
(d. 1925)

William II,
Kaiser of
Germany
(d. 1941)

Albert Victor,
Duke of
Clarence
(d. 1892)

GEORGE V
(r. 1910-36)
m.
Mary of
Teck
(d. 1953)

Louise,
Princess Royal
(d. 1931)
m.
Alexander
Duff,
Duke of Fife
(d. 1912)

EDWARD VIII
(r. 1936, d. 1972)
m.
Wallis
Warfield
(Mrs Simpson)

GEORGE VI
(r. 1936-52)
m.
Elizabeth
Bowes-Lyon

Mary,
Princess Royal
(d. 1965)
m.
Henry
Lascelles,
Earl of Harewood
(d. 1947)

Henry,
Duke of
Gloucester
m.
Alice
Montague-
Douglas-
Scott

Margaret m. Antony
Armstrong-Jones,
Earl of Snowdon

David,
Viscount Linley

Sarah

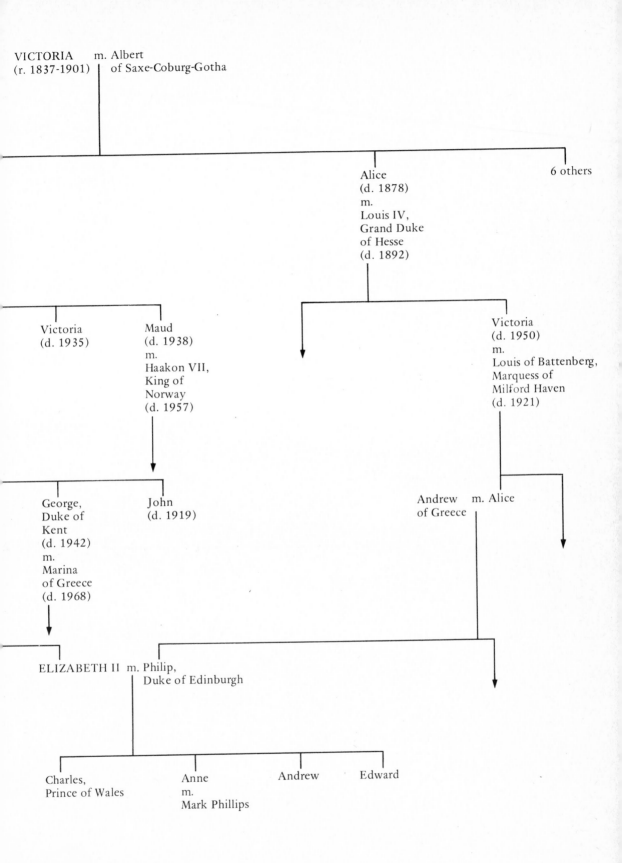

VICTORIA   m. Albert
(r. 1837-1901)   of Saxe-Coburg-Gotha

Alice
(d. 1878)
m.
Louis IV,
Grand Duke
of Hesse
(d. 1892)

6 others

Victoria
(d. 1935)

Maud
(d. 1938)
m.
Haakon VII,
King of
Norway
(d. 1957)

Victoria
(d. 1950)
m.
Louis of Battenberg,
Marquess of
Milford Haven
(d. 1921)

George,
Duke of
Kent
(d. 1942)
m.
Marina
of Greece
(d. 1968)

John
(d. 1919)

Andrew   m. Alice
of Greece

ELIZABETH II m. Philip,
            Duke of Edinburgh

Charles,
Prince of Wales

Anne
m.
Mark Phillips

Andrew

Edward

Select bibliography

MONARCHY

Aubrey Buxton, *The King in his Country*, 1955.
Harold Nicolson, *King George V, his Life and Reign*, 1952.
Sir Charles Petrie, *Monarchy in the Twentieth Century*, 1952.
Sir John W. Wheeler-Bennett, *King George VI, his Life and Reign*, 1958.
HRH Duke of Windsor, *A King's Story*, 1957.

BIOGRAPHY AND MEMOIRS

C. R. Attlee, *As It Happened*, 1954.
Lord Birkenhead, *Life of Lord Halifax*, 1965.
Alan Bullock, *Life and Times of Ernest Bevin*, (2 vols).
'Chips', *The Diaries of Sir Henry Channon* (edited R. V. R. James, 1967).
Hugh Dalton, *The Fateful Years, 1941–5*, 1957.
J. C. C. Dividson, *Memoirs of a Conservative* (edited R. V. R. James, 1969).
Keith Feiling, *Neville Chamberlain*, 1946.
Thomas Jones, *Diary with letters 1931–50*, 1954.
Harold Macmillan, *Tides of Fortune, 1945–55*, 1969.
R. K. Middlemas, and A. J. L. Barnes, *Baldwin*, 1969.
Harold Nicolson, *Diaries and Letters*, (2 volumes) 1966–68.

GENERAL – FOREIGN, HOME AND COMMONWEALTH AFFAIRS

C. J. Bartlett, *The Long Retreat*, 1969.
S. H. Beer, *Modern British Politics*, 1965.
B. G. Gilbert, *British Social Policy, 1914–38*, 1970.
Gabriel Kolko, *Politics of War, 1943–45*, 1968.
Norman Longmate, *How We Lived Then*, 1971.
Nicholas Mansergh, *The Commonwealth Experience*, 1969.
D. C. Marsh, *The Changing Social Structure of England and Wales*, 1958.
W. M. Medlicott, *British Foreign Policy Since Versailles*, 1968.
C. L. Mowat, *Britain Between the Wars, 1918–40*, 1955.
F. S. Northedge, *British Foreign Policy, 1945–61*, 1962.
Michael Sissons and Philip French, *The Age of Austerity 1945–51*, 1963.
A. J. P. Taylor, *English History, 1914–45*, 1965.
G. M. Worswick, *The British Economy, 1945–59*, 1967.

Index